I0422191

THE SELF TAUGHT BAKER BUSINESS BLUEPRINT

MASTERING MINDSET, SKILLS AND STRATEGY TO BUILD A 6-FIGURE BAKING BUSINESS

BY:

ALANA HOLAS

Foreword

Dear Readers,

It is with great joy and pride that I have the privilege to introduce you to a masterful guide penned by an impeccable entrepreneur and an exceptional cake artist, Alana Ada Holas. As the Executive Assistant to Alana, I have witnessed firsthand the creativity, dedication and unwavering commitment she pours into her craft.

This book is not just a guide; it's a journey through her 16 years showing the ins and outs of running a successful cake business. From her early days of experimenting with flavors in her kitchen with family and friends to the bad ass cake decorator that Alana is today, this book encapsulates all the wisdom and insights garnered along the way.

In this book, Alana shares the secrets, the trials, and the triumphs that have shaped her into the force in the cake industry that she is today. With each page turned, you'll find yourself not only immersed in the technicalities of baking, decorating systems and processes but you will also be captivated by the entrepreneurial spirit that propels her business forward.

Running a cake business isn't just about sugar, flour and decor; it's about understanding your pricing, knowing when and where to implement steps to fast track your business, and navigating your entrepreneurial goals. Alana doesn't just take you step by step through stepping up your business backends ; she imparts invaluable lessons on the importance of your mindset, resilience, customer relations, marketing strategies, and the art of paying yourself.

To the aspiring bakers, the dreamers contemplating if they are good enough to start, or those seeking to elevate their existing cake business—prepare to embark on a journey that transcends any other baker business book. This is a manual crafted from real-world experience, where every tip and piece of advice is a gem earned through the experience of building and sustaining a thriving custom cake business.

As you dive into the pages ahead, visualize Alana as your experienced mentor, guiding you through the intricacies of the cake business world. May this book equip you, inspire you, and light a motivational flame within, just as it has for the countless clients and students who have experienced the magic of Alana.

Whether professionally through A's Exquisite Cakes, Baking It Academy or socially association as a friend or loved one Alana has successfully managed to improve the lives of anyone willing to listen.

Here's to taking the leap as you set out on this fulfilling baking journey, and to the endless possibilities that await you within the pages of this remarkable book.

Sincerely,

Shadé Mckenzie
Executive Assistant to Alana Holas

Acknowledgement

For Dad

While every cake holds a special place in my heart, the process of creating wedding cakes with my family is a cherished tradition that I hold dear.

Years ago, when our dad fell ill, juggling hospital visits and doctor appointments left me struggling to keep up with weekend orders, staring at the possibility of several sleepless nights. One evening, after our nightly hospital visit, my sisters surprised me by showing up at my doorstep. Margaret assisted with baking, Gillian took charge of the dishes, kept me organized, and even assembled my very first emergency delivery kit (complete with an electric kettle, of all things—turns out, we did need it). Eulanda or "Tix" as we call her, helped with sugar flowers and final preparations for the weekend.

As the years passed, this tradition evolved to include Dad handling the dishes (he jokingly called himself the Chief Cook and Bottle Washer) and providing us with laughter. Gillian continued to keep me on schedule, and Margaret, who now resides in Atlanta, joined us on our journey via telephone as Fabian drove us to our destination.

This tradition allows me to focus solely on crafting the wedding cake, free from worries about potential crises, as my family stands by me and handles any challenges that arise.

As a family, we always conclude our adventure by gathering at a restaurant to relax, eat, and reflect on our day.

I cherish this tradition dearly and miss it profoundly when circumstances prevent us from coming together. I often wonder if those occasions when we can't all be present lose a bit of their magic.

Happy birthday, Daddy.

Rest in eternal peace

Contents

CHAPTER 1: CULTIVATING A BAKER'S MINDSET

Welcome to a journey of transformation, where your mindset shapes not just your cakes, but your entire baking business. This chapter dives into how a shift in thinking can lead to substantial growth and success, especially for self-taught bakers and cake decorators.

"She is expensive"

From the start my cakes were always considered to be expensive, yet I was making 6 to 7 cakes per week plus cupcakes and cookies.

I was also averaging 2 hours of sleep per night and still wasn't able to cover my bills.

This was a wake-up call about pricing - but it wasn't just about numbers; it was about believing in the value of my creations and understanding my worth.

Herein lies the first lesson in mindset: your self-worth sets the stage for your financial success.

So many people walk around saying "work on your mindset", "develop a growth mindset' or "mindset is everything". It all sounds so easy right?

However very few are willing to actually tell you exactly how that can be done.

As bakers and self-taught bakers, how we think about ourselves and what we can accomplish can have a great impact on how we perform; at work, while building our business and in our daily lives. Despite knowing this, we rarely take into consideration how often we negatively think or speak about ourselves and our abilities.

"I am a badass cake designer!! I am a badass cake designer!!". I repeated that phrase to myself over and over for months until I believed it with all of my heart and soul. Now I can easily work the sentence "I am a badass cake designer" in any conversation when introducing myself. Ask yourself the following questions; How would I like to be known? Do I need to work on believing it myself before others will?

Developing and fostering a better mindset for yourself will by no means be easy. Many assume that you just say a few daily positive affirmations and your mindset changes but contrary to popular beliefs it is so much more than that, I repeated the mantra daily but I also practiced my craft relentlessly.

Teaching yourself to speak positively about your work, business and daily life can be difficult especially when your mind is resisting and telling you it just isn't so. You have to learn to push past the initial resistance and work daily to create the mindset that will help you build the life and business you desire.

By this point you might be wondering what mindsets are. Mindset is a series of self-beliefs that determine your behavior, outlook and overall mental attitude. For example, believing you are either 'good at cake decorating' or 'bad at cake decorating' will actually affect your skill, how you work and how much you're willing to grow your business.

Fixed vs Growth Mindset. Which one are you?

A Fixed mindset individual is very stuck in their way and not very open to changes. They tend to avoid challenges and feel threatened when others succeed. They also believe their characteristics are fixed traits and that a person succeeds or fails based solely on talent. They spend most of their time focusing on and documenting their intelligence or talent instead of developing them.

A growth mindset individual on the other hand believes that their most basic abilities can be developed through dedication and hard work—brains and talent are just the starting point. "This view creates a love of learning and a resilience that is essential for great accomplishment." (Dweck, 2015)

Our mindset shapes how we view the world and ourselves by influencing how we think, feel, and behave in any given situation. Meaning what you believe about yourself will in turn impact if you succeed or fail. For example, believing that taking additional classes and courses or practicing your skill will make you better while simultaneously helping you evolve and grow your cake business is your mindset setting you up for success.

You may be wondering, if a person has a fixed mindset is it possible to change or work to develop a growth mindset? The short answer is yes!

A growth mindset or success mindset is a skill and can be worked on and developed like any other. We have the ability to change from a fixed to a growth mindset if we are willing to put in the work necessary to change, starting with awareness of your current mindset.

Seven Essential Mindset Principles for Every Baker to Master

1. Learning to manage stress and maintain a positive attitude. Stress can be a major obstacle to success and it is important to find effective ways to manage it. This can include things like exercise, meditation, or other stress-relief techniques. Additionally, maintaining a positive attitude can help you stay motivated and focused on your goals.

2. Learning to be patient. Growing a business takes time and it is important to have the patience to see it through. This means being willing to put in the work and make sacrifices in the short-term for long-term success.

3. Learning to be adaptable. Running a business often requires making quick decisions and adjusting to changing circumstances. It is important to be open to new ideas and be willing to adapt to new strategies and approaches.

4. Learning to be self-motivated. Running a business can be lonely, and it can be easy to lose motivation. Successful business owners find ways to stay motivated and focused on their goals, even when things get tough.

5. Learning to be self-disciplined. Running a business requires a lot of hard work and dedication, and it is important to have the discipline to put in the work and stay focused on your goals.

6. Learning to be self-confident. Running a business can be challenging, and it is important to have the confidence to make decisions, take risks, and overcome obstacles

7. Learning to be resilient. Running a business can be challenging and there will be times when you face obstacles and setbacks. It is

important to have the mental toughness to push through these tough times and come out stronger on the other side.

Release past caking failures and move forward.

People are often so very quick to tell you to let it go and move on. Can it be that easy? One key aspect of developing a successful mindset is learning to embrace failure as a learning opportunity. When things don't go as planned, it can be easy to get discouraged and give up on your goals. However, successful business owners understand that failure is an inevitable part of the process and use it as a learning opportunity to improve and grow.

Reflect on past wins. The cakes that you have created that made you say "I can't believe I made that" or the times in your daily life where you have exceeded your own expectations. Focus on channeling those feelings whenever you think you are incapable of accomplishing your current tasks. Then I challenge you to reflect on the mistake. Examine it from every angle and figure out ways that it could have been prevented or corrected. View it as a learning experience, take the lessons, let go and move forward.

I know this can be easier said than done. You may have to talk yourself through the process by telling yourself over and over that you made a mistake but you are not your mistake.

Focus on channeling your past wins, couple them with the lessons that you learnt and remind yourself that others before you have failed and pushed past the failures to build amazing cake businesses and so can you. You're building a positive mindset muscle and with time you will be able to work through failures faster, always taking the lessons, letting go and moving forward.

Learn how to utilize negative client feedback in the best way.

In order to grow and make your business better you need to seek feedback from others. Clients past and present as well as people that can be trusted to be fair, truthful and provide honest feedback without looking to spare your feelings.

Sometimes feedback can be hard to hear. Take your feelings out of it. It's not personal. Put your grown up pants on and correct the mistakes you're making, get your business on the right path. I am saying this to you while sitting in the middle of feedback that made me just want to curl up in a corner and contemplate my life choices. However my mindset would not allow that. Instead I will sit in my feelings for a while then I will dust myself off and try again. It took a lot of work and self-awareness to build this mindset but now it's just who I am.

Fixed mindset individuals on the other hand, view negative feedback as a confirmation of all their fears. While growth mindset individuals welcome the feedback and recognize it as the gift that it is. They acknowledge that it will help them to make changes within their business. It's important to remember that how we think and speak about ourselves matters. We can change our own narrative, when you hear yourself speaking negatively about yourself and your life, shut it down, change it to the positive version of that statement. Remember building your mindset is like building a muscle, consistent repetition is key.

Mindset Maintenance

Rest and relaxation is the best thing that you can do for your mind and your business. As a small business owner it's often hard to process downtime. Even when we're so tired that we're basically dead on our feet the idea of a weekend free can cause intense panic and terror.

One of the hardest mindset shifts I had to make as a business owner was moving away from taking every single cake order. I had to learn how many orders I could optimally fit within the workweek and over deliver on those.

That meant moving away from last minute orders and focusing instead on providing value to the clients that placed timely orders by over-delivering and planning in optimal time to rest.

Allowing time for rest makes it possible for our body to recharge and our body and mind to function optimally at peak during the work week and our daily lives.

Learn to relax. Give yourself time and space so that your brain isn't constantly on the go. Avoid negative conversations with others whenever possible. Think about how much you complain and how much you listen to the complaints of others. These negative interactions drain our energy and make it impossible to relax. Focus instead on the positive; this helps you build a positive mindset.

Common Business Mindset issues we face as self-taught bakers

Difficulty with pricing: The main issue that self-taught bakers and bakers may face difficulty with is pricing their products. Set clear financial goals that can help you in this area. By determining your desired profit margin, you can set prices that will allow you to achieve your financial goals while still being competitive.

My online pricing course will help you to overcome all your pricing issues.

Get Pricing like a pro https://www.bakingitacademy.com/pricinglikeapro

30% discount code: SBBB

Difficulty with time management: Many self-taught bakers and bakers struggle with managing their time effectively, leading to stress and burnout. To overcome this issue, it's important for you to develop self-discipline and establish a schedule for completing tasks. Prioritizing important tasks while delegating some of the work to others can help with time management.

Difficulty with marketing: Another common issue that self-taught bakers and bakers may face is difficulty with marketing their business. This can be overcome by being adaptable and open to new ideas. Consider experimenting with different marketing strategies, such as social media, networking events or even utilizing influencers.

Difficulty with creativity: Self-taught bakers and bakers may also face difficulty with coming up with new and creative ideas for their products. To overcome this, try to be patient, embrace failure and learn from it, try new techniques and don't be afraid to ask for feedback from others.

Difficulty with scaling: Scaling a business can be difficult and self-taught bakers and bakers may not know where to start. To overcome this, set clear goals, be adaptable, and be willing to make sacrifices in the short-term for long-term success. It may also be useful to seek advice from others who have successfully scaled their businesses.

Difficulty with consistency: Consistency in taste, design and quality is very important for bakers and bakers to maintain their reputation. To overcome this, you can use self-motivation, self-discipline and have a system in place for measuring and maintaining quality.

Difficulty maintaining industry standards: You may not have the same understanding of industry standards and expectations as those with formal training. This can be overcome by researching and learning about industry standards, and seeking out feedback from customers and industry professionals.

Personal Mindset issues we face as self-taught bakers

Self-doubt: You may have a lack of formal training or education in the field, which can lead to feelings of self-doubt. This can be overcome by developing self-confidence and embracing failure as a learning opportunity. Remind yourself of your past successes, and the progress you have made, it will give you the confidence to move forward.

Fear of failure: You may be more likely to fear failure due to lack of formal training or education. This can be overcome by setting clear goals and using failure as a learning opportunity to improve and grow.

Isolation: You may not have the same network of peers and mentors that those with formal training have. This can lead to feelings of isolation and can be overcome by networking and seeking out other self-taught bakers and bakers for support and advice.

By being aware of these unique mindset issues, self-taught bakers and bakers can take steps to overcome them and develop the mindset necessary to grow their business.

Money Mindset

I changed the entire landscape of my business with a $2,000 sugar flower class

When this class initially launched. They reached out to me and offered a $400 discount. I couldn't afford it. I was $16,000 in debt and my constant mantra to myself was Lord Jesus how will I ever pay this off.

They offered the class again a few months later. They added a payment plan through Klarna. I applied and was approved and booked the class instantly.

Roughly 2 weeks before the world went into lock down we completed the 3 day class and honestly everything about it was amazing to me. She taught us the fundamental techniques that we could apply to the making of any flower instead of focusing on teaching just a small cross section of flowers.

After the world went into lockdown I was determined to keep our regular schedule for myself, my fiancé Fabian and our kids. I walked 45 minutes to my studio everyday, stealing flowers all the way there.

I practiced everything I learnt in my class from Monday to Friday. At the end of lockdown I had an entire new collection of modern sugar flower wedding cake designs.

This catapulted my business in the direction I desired. It allowed me to niche down, dial in to my ideal clients, reduce the number of orders I produced while making easily 2-3 times more per cake than I did before.

Like I said it drastically changed the landscape of my business.

Is there a class, or course that can do that for your business? What area would you choose to focus? How drastically will this class change your business? Your future? The number of hours you work?

Major turning points in your life and business

Until last year $2000 had been the single highest individual investment I had made in my business.

I joined the Goal Accelerator Club a few years ago. One of the courses they offer is the "7 Day Vision Unlock". That course was almost my undoing. It showed me a path for my future and business that scared the shit out of me. Everything I thought would take center stage, larger events, more weddings, more expensive cakes was taking a back seat to everything that I previously thought would be secondary, teaching other self-taught bakers like myself to stretch themselves, strive for more and become obsessed with constantly transforming their business and skill.

I attended a retreat hosted by the founder of the club. It's important to note that this would be my first retreat. For me it was a week of extreme growth, and an awakening to the possibility of a future that I never even knew I wanted or longed for.

It was during this retreat, that I personally met my now business strategist and mentor.

I'm not going to lie, I stalked her. Every time she turned around I was just there. Finally she gave up, guys I wore her down she said, "ok, ok give me a week to decompress from this retreat because it was a lot then we will set up a discovery call" (did I mention that she was the mastermind of the retreat i was attending) "ok" i said. OMG I was over the moon. Help was finally in sight.

During our discovery call I realized that she was not in fact going to recommend someone but was going to work with me herself. My body did something on the inside that I can't really explain but my face remained calm. I know that because I looked at the camera and well it didn't show. I was proud of that.

That call was followed by a proposal detailing what was involved in working with her and of course the cost. Even though I was tempted to scroll straight to the price I made myself read through the proposal. It was just everything. I had never so clearly seen in black and white everything I wanted for my business, not to mention the things that I had never even thought was possible. It was all laid out step by step right there.

Back to the cost...It's worth mentioning that up until this point I just stared at the proposal amount in silence, contemplating how to raise the $28,000 needed. My friend Kedisha, bombarded me with questions, but ultimately encouraged me to pursue what I desired. She stressed the importance of making a decision and acting on it.

My second big test would come the next day when my assistant Shade got her very first look at the proposal. She, like Fabian, has entire conversations with their facial expressions that are totally at odds with the words that come out of their mouths and I really, really needed the honesty of face to face. What happened instead made me cry. In fact, I'm sitting here crying just thinking about it. She looked me in the eye and said I have $1000 in the bank that I can give to you, it's not a loan, it's a gift, you don't have to pay me back.

Pivotal moments happen in your life but you have to be ready for them. If I had not been in the middle of a mindset shift, had not been at a retreat that opened me further, helped me build unforgettable connections with other strong women, if my views about my future had not drastically changed during that week. I would not have been in the right mindset to say yes to this proposal and commit wholeheartedly to a path that would change my business and eventually change my life.

Purposely seek challenges to strengthen your mindset and skill.

Say yes to opportunity.

There may be an area that you're looking to grow, or a direction that you would like to take in your business but you just don't think you're ready. If an opportunity in that area presents itself, seize it, because chances are you will never feel ready.

You will never be able to grow if you're always comfortable, this causes you to stagnate, push past your comfort level and growth will occur.

My fellow baker, what are you blocking, what are you preventing or allowing to hold you back, shift your mindset, accept the path that God has set just for you. Join me and commit to your business and your life. Make the changes that will take both not just to the next level but to the next stratosphere.

Visualization as a mindset building strategy

As bakers and self-taught bakers it is important to make the most of our imagination. Did you know that your brain doesn't know the difference between a real experience and a vividly imagined experience. I don't mean a mediocre visualization, I mean walking through the process step by step. Imagine how it would feel, how it would smell, how you will feel after it's completed and you realize that you were able to accomplish something that you never thought was possible. How would people react to you? What will they say? Imagine it all, get as detailed as possible, know that initially your brain will resist and tell you that it's not real, push past that feeling, i promise you that over time it will become easier.

Six years ago a mentor asked me, "What kind of storefront do you want?" The question made me pause, what do you mean? I just want a storefront, it's what everyone wants. Yes, she responded but what does a storefront mean to you? It's crazy I know but in 10 years no one had ever asked me what I wanted and more importantly I had never asked it of myself.

I really took this to heart, I went home and sat quietly with myself and the list of questions she had asked me. After working through them I realized that the storefront and business I wanted wasn't what I had been working towards and looked nothing like the traditional bakery storefront.

Visualization exercise

- What is your equivalent of a storefront?
- What does it look like?
- How does it smell?
- How do you want customers to feel when they walk in the door?
- How will you greet them?
- What experience do you want them to have?
- How would you like it to be decorated?
- What colors do you want to paint the walls?
- How do you want it to be furnished?
- How will the showroom look?
- What equipment will you have in the decorating space?
- What do you want to bake there?
- What cakes do YOU want to create there?
- How will you feel once they are created?
- How will your clients react to seeing and tasting the finished products?
- What will they say?
- How will you feel?

Pause now and do this exercise

Use the information to create your lists of goals. Taking one goal at a time and making sub-goals then use those sub goals to create tasks.

Make the tasks as small as possible and work daily crossing off small tasks as you go.

It doesn't matter how or where you start, start now, start scared, start where you are with what you have and work toward a larger GOAL.

Some of the most important lessons that I have learnt over the past 16 years. Pay attention to how you think and speak about your life, self and business.

Words have power. Speak and work towards positive outcomes. Refuse to complain or listen to others complain.

Get to work, learn, practice and implement.

Take absolute responsibility for your life and the skill and business that you are building. How you think about yourself will directly determine how much you can build and grow your cake business.

CHAPTER 2: BUILDING RESILIENCE AND PERSISTENCE

The Marathon of Building a Sustainable Cake Business: Beyond Initial Enthusiasm

Starting a cake business is often fueled by a burst of enthusiasm. You're brimming with ideas about colors, fonts, and a heart full of passion for the entrepreneurial journey ahead. However, transforming this vision into a sustainably strong, profitable, and scalable business is more of a marathon than a sprint, demanding immense dedication and effort.

In the early stages, motivation is your driving force, propelling you through the excitement of turning plans into reality. Yet, the real test begins when this initial enthusiasm wanes, leaving you to face the day-to-day, often mundane realities of running a business. It's during these phases that many entrepreneurs experience delays or even setbacks in their business growth.

As you navigate the ups and downs of building your cake business, it's persistence that becomes your lifeline, especially when you see other cake businesses seemingly flourishing. In moments of doubt, questioning your next step or pondering your strategy, it's resilience that fuels your belief in success. This resilience is what allows you to wake up each morning with the conviction that success is attainable, and that perseverance is key to reaching brighter days ahead.

Persistence is the energy that drives you to reevaluate and adapt your plans, pushing you forward even when the path seems unclear. Learning to identify and harness these qualities - resilience and persistence - not only bolsters your resolve but also significantly enhances your productivity.

In the world of cake entrepreneurship, where passion meets practicality, it's these qualities that differentiate those who endure and thrive from those who falter. Embrace this journey with resilience and persistence, and watch as your cake business flourishes into a sustainable, profitable venture.

An Unforeseen Journey: From Dental School Aspirant to Cake Decorating Entrepreneur

Cake decorating was never a part of my original career plan. When I immigrated to the USA from Grenada, I didn't have a clear career trajectory in mind. My friend Lorian's suggestion was to go to dental school seemed like a viable path, and I dived into it wholeheartedly, balancing a full-time job as a legal secretary and weekend cleaning gigs alongside my biology major studies.

However, my journey took an unexpected turn when my sister Margaret tasked me with making a sweet 16 cake for my niece, Allissa. Baking was a skill imparted by our parents, but cake decorating was uncharted territory. I spent months learning through online videos, grappling with techniques like butter-creaming, fondant covering, and flower placement – a world away from my dental school applications.

The experience of creating that cake, despite its imperfections, ignited a passion in me for baking and cake decorating. It was the joy and bonding it brought to my family that made it my favorite project. This newfound love gradually shifted my focus entirely, leading me to make a bold decision in the midst of my dental school applications: I would turn my passion for cakes into a business.

My family and friends, expecting me to pursue a career in dentistry, were disappointed and disapproving. Despite the growth of my business, the skills I developed, and the income I generated, they saw it merely as a hobby, urging me to return to school. Their doubts only fueled my determination to succeed.

Persisting through the toughest times, from the fatigue of back-to-back tasks to the days when everything seemed to go awry, I clung to my resilience. Now, as I look around my studio, reflecting on the array of display and event cakes I've created, I'm filled with gratitude for the skills I've honed. Thinking back to my early struggles, I marvel at how far I've come. If someone had told me 16 years ago that I would build a business and brand that fills me with pride, I would have scarcely believed it.

Strategies for building these traits

Resilience is the ability to bounce back from life's challenges and it's a vital skill to foster for long-term success. It is important to be resilient and persistent in life and in business. Train yourself to deal with the challenges that come with running a business on a daily basis.

In order for this to be effective I need to show you that I have been where you are. I have built traits that allow me to move past the things that happen daily, that could derail the future of my business and I promise you that I have stories in abundance. The thing is, I no longer allow the mistakes, missteps and bad moments to drive the narrative of my story, my life or business.

Resilience is a skill that can be built like any other. Here are a few ways that you can build and use it in your daily life and business.

Learn from the experience by turning setbacks into opportunities for growth.

Examine the situation from every angle. What was the expected outcome? How did it differ from the actual outcome? What went wrong? Was it one particular thing or a series of events? What went as planned? Was the mistake preventable? What steps can be taken next time to prevent its occurrence? Is there a particular skill that can be learnt and implemented?

Experiencing rough patches as business owners often reveals that you're stronger than you thought. Resilience gives you the ability to rise to the occasion and learn new skills. The experience can enhance your appreciation for life and remind you to be thankful for what you have.

Change how you respond to situations

While there will be circumstances that are beyond your control like illness and natural disasters you can change how you respond to difficult situations. Be decisive and proactive. When problems and tasks become overwhelming it's helpful to break them into smaller, more manageable pieces and focus on one thing at a time. Taking initiative and building consistency can help you stay on track even when you're no longer motivated, giving you a sense of purpose during stressful times.

Maintaining your health and taking care of yourself

Oftentimes situations both expected and unexpected can cause stress which can affect us physically and emotionally. Maintaining a healthy lifestyle can strengthen your body and help build a strong foundation for resilience and emotional wellbeing.

It is important to give yourself the resources you need to stay strong. Eat a healthy diet. Get enough sleep. Exercise regularly. Stay hydrated. Avoid unhealthy coping mechanisms, like alcohol or other substances. Find time to relax, whether through meditation, yoga, prayer, deep breathing exercises, or journaling. Whichever outlet works best for you

Build and maintain strong relationships

Creating relationships either virtual or in person provide support that helps you to feel connected to something larger than yourself and can provide you with so much to look forward to. Connect with family members, friends, community groups both online and in person, try to find people who share your interests. You can develop these connections by getting involved in local groups, taking a class to improve your skill, joining a church or organization of your choosing. These relationships serve as a reminder that we're not alone. I have so many that are near and dear to me and they started on social media. I met many of them in my women empowerment group Goal Accelerator. Women that have now become like sisters, who I can call on in times of celebration or heartache, and they will always be ready, willing and able to discuss next steps.

Positivity over negativity

During the mindset chapter we discussed the significance of monitoring our thoughts and maintaining a positive outlook. It's hard to feel hopeful when life isn't going your way. Your mindset plays a key role in your ability to get back on your feet after being knocked down. When you learn to build resilience you're less likely to focus on problems, and feel taken advantage of or overwhelmed for extended periods of time. You develop the ability to bounce back faster as you are more likely to accept that change is part of life.

Set Small, Achievable Goals

Establishing goals that are specific, measurable, and timely can help you to stay on track, be resilient and persist during the most challenging times. Talk about your goals with like-minded people. This will hold you accountable and help you to create a network of support resilient.

Focus on the Journey, Not the Outcome

Continuously obsessing over the end result, whether it be success or failure, can significantly dampen motivation and cause you to overlook the significance of the journey. Remember to celebrate the victories, small and large, along the way. This helps keep you motivated and working toward larger goals. Additionally, don't be afraid to make mistakes along your journey as they are lessons that provide opportunities for you to improve and grow.

Practice Gratitude

Gratitude helps you to be constantly aware of who or what you have to be thankful for. It also reminds you of all the resources you have during stressful or challenging times. Practice gratitude by writing down everything you have to be thankful for at the end or beginning of each day. This small activity can motivate you to keep going.

At every stage in my career there have been people who have believed in me even when I didn't believe in myself. People who made it possible for me to continue on my journey until I believed in myself. Those who show up for me wholeheartedly like my fiancé Fabian who would stay up late with me until I finish my orders instead of going to bed after a long day of work. My friend Nikki, who accompanies me to deliveries whenever she can. She is also the reason why I get random phone calls from people wanting to order chocolate cake with cookies and cream filling because she raved to them about how good it is. My friend, mentor and coach Abeiki who was the first person to ask me "What does a storefront mean to me?" She is also the person who pulled me out of my shell and encouraged me to start networking. Of course by "encouraged" I mean she dragged me to multiple events. I am grateful for them and so many more like them. These are people who have held space for me and allowed me to be fully myself even when I didn't understand who that was yet.

Strike a balance

This almost ended my business and would have made me never want to make another cake.

For years I worked around the clock in my business. The issue was never finding time to work but finding time to do anything else. For years work was my sole focus. I didn't realize the control it had taken over my life until after the birth of my son Christian. When taking care of his basic needs meant taking time away from current cake projects. While feeding, bathing or just spending time with him I would be constantly going over lists in my head of all the things I had left to do for the week. I never just allowed myself to enjoy motherhood, like the moments with my babies or to just be present. It was always how fast I could get back to work.

I returned to work one month after giving birth to my son and three weeks after having my daughter. My body was in constant pain, my lower back ache and my feet were constantly swollen. I went to bed tired and after a few short hours woke up tired. It was a vicious cycle. My assistant Shade grew increasingly concerned and started suggesting that I lay down, sit down or just take breaks.

I remember being on the verge of passing out one day and overhearing her on the phone with my fiancé Fabian.

Work life balance for me just didn't exist and it was starting to not only affect me but everyone around me.

A few months after that day my body crashed and just refused to do what I asked. I had to stop taking orders. I tried to sleep but I was so conditioned to operate on little to no sleep that I found it impossible. I sat up in the dark for hours while everyone else in the house slept peacefully. When I did sleep, I woke drenched in sweat and the bed would be soaked. I grew increasingly conscious of the fact that while on hiatus from work, my bills still had to be paid and I was blowing through my savings. My passion for baking and all things cake decorating was literally killing me.

As I'm sitting here writing this book I'm obviously still alive so let's discuss how I overcame the hardest hurdle to date in my professional career as a baker. First I consulted with my primary care physician. It would take multiple doctors to help me work back to a place where I felt even remotely normal in my body and mind. I started taking custom vitamins, I restarted a daily workout routine and got a trainer. I had a very open discussion with him about my life up to that point and the body I wanted to build going forward. I started meal prepping and eating actual meals, ensured that they were healthy and nourished my body. Lastly, I went back to therapy. Therapy helped me realize that I was on a hamster wheel in my business, I was constantly working on it and did not allow myself to work on it. My goal of growing my business would remain a goal because I was not working toward achieving it. I was in fact an employee in my business and not its CEO. The business was in fact running me and no one was running it, charting a course for growth, expansion or additional streams of income.

With the realization that I needed to work on my business and not just on my business, I did some soul searching in order to figure out what I wanted for my business and my life. Really deep dive into what was possible for my business and not just what I was always told was possible.

First I transitioned my business from general to wedding cakes. Then I added a specialty or niche with the addition of sugar flowers and making modern sugar flower wedding cake designs. Customer experience and customer service became pivotal to me and creating those experiences for clients became the messaging. To regain my time I created systems and processes in my business, figured out how many cakes I could optimally produce in a week and stuck to that number. To buy back my freedom I deep dived into pricing, figuring out what I should and shouldn't be charging for and positioning my business to price for profit. My life now is unrecognizable for what it was just a few short years ago. I am grateful everyday that my passion for my work is returning and that I can now pursue it in a healthier way.

The business I want is possible now! This lesson freed me. Attending a sugar flower workshop was a transformative experience. The mentor I met there reshaped my understanding of what was possible in my cake business. Contrary to my previous belief that a large storefront and team were necessary for success, she demonstrated that a small, efficient team could achieve remarkable results. When necessary for larger cakes or time consuming orders she hired freelance bakers. Yes there is such a thing as freelance bakers. This insight was a game-changer, showing me that the business and life I desired were within reach.

This journey taught me that the dream business doesn't have to take years to build. It starts with understanding what you truly want, finding mentors who have achieved similar goals, learning from them, and charting your own path. Now, as I reflect on the growth and success of my business, I am grateful for the lessons learned and the balance I have found.

Harnessing Motivation and Affirmations for Success in Your Cake Business

Motivation is the driving force that propels us toward our goals and dreams. It's that internal spark compelling us to take action, overcome challenges, and persevere even in adversity. Whether aiming for career success, personal development, or excellence in leadership, motivation is crucial in your journey to greatness.

To tap into this vital force, consider these key insights:

Power of Affirmations and Positive Thinking

Affirmations, coupled with a positive outlook, have the potential to transform both your life and your cake business. While affirmations alone are not a magic solution, they are powerful when combined with dedicated effort. Initially, I borrowed affirmations from mentors, adapting them to my personal context. Gradually, I learned to craft my own, tailored to my aspirations and business.

You might be skeptical about the impact of affirmations and positive thinking on your cake business, but I assure you, embracing these practices can revolutionize your mindset, planning, and future outlook.

Crafting Personalized Affirmations

To create effective affirmations, start by envisioning your dream life and business. What does it encompass? How do you spend your days, what activities bring you joy, and who are the people sharing your life? Reflecting on these aspects will guide you in formulating affirmations that resonate with your goals.

Affirmations for Cake Business Success

- "I am destined for greatness and success in my cake business."
- "My business will thrive and prosper."
- "I possess the skills and knowledge necessary to achieve my goals."
- "I am a confident and capable leader."
- "Each day, my business grows stronger and more resilient."
- "I welcome challenges as opportunities for growth."
- "I attract loyal and supportive clients."

- "My actions are in harmony with my business vision and objectives."
- "I am dedicated to constant learning and improvement."
- "My mindset is attuned to financial prosperity."
- Overcoming Self-Doubt with Affirmations:
- "I trust in my ability to succeed in my cake business."
- "Success and opportunity are my rightful claims."
- "I am equipped to thrive in my business endeavors."
- "Challenges are opportunities for learning and growth."
- "My past experiences are stepping stones to future success."
- "I confidently promote my products and expertise."
- "Fear does not limit my potential."
- "I am worthy of financial success and abundance."
- "I replace negative thoughts with empowering affirmations."

These examples illustrate how affirmations can be tailored to your specific needs and goals. Repeat them daily, and witness the transformative power they can bring to your life and business.

Encouragement and advice for persistence

For as long as I can remember I have always had the need to "try one more time" as home bakers and cake decorators often with no professional training so many things go wrong. We're often in a constant state of overwhelm or stress trying to fix the things that we break on a daily basis. Learn to be patient with yourself and give yourself grace. Understand that there is always a learning curve and everything gets better with time and practice.

We often think that as home bakers we need to operate in a constant state of motivation. However if we create systems, processes and schedules for our business we can operate in a state of consistency when motivation has deserted us. It allows us to keep our business running and to keep working towards our goals.

"Success leaves clues". As home bakers and cake decorators living in the social media age we are constantly bombarded with a litany of other bakers who seem so much more successful or creative that we are. I encourage you not to compare your skill or creativity but to take a look at their business model, learn from them, what's working for them? Can a version of that work for you and your business? How are they showing up for their business and community? Can you emulate that consistency in your business? Take the clues left by their successes and implement it to create a better business model for your business.

CHAPTER 3: STARTING YOUR BAKING BUSINESS

Running a profitable home bakery business is so much more than making pretty cakes and developing your skill. In order to grow, scale and actually be profitable you have to become good at all aspects of your business including, purchasing insurance coverage, and learning to market and network. These are general guidelines; however, given the regional variations in laws, it's crucial to consult with your local food and business regulatory agencies before proceeding.

Making sure you're legally set

Operating a bakery from home means that you're running a business, thereby making it accountable to adhere to state and local regulations governing details such as food, business licensing, and taxes. Furthermore, there are specific laws that pertain to the sale of food products from a residential building, this adds an additional layer of complexity to the legalities of running a home bakery business. We're providing you with general guidelines; however, given the regional variations in laws, it's crucial to consult with your local food and business regulatory agencies before proceeding with your home bakery.

Know and understand your cottage food laws

Home bakery businesses typically fall under a legal category called cottage food. This classification distinguishes home-based bakeries from commercial or retail establishments which operate out of dedicated storefronts or production kitchens. While commercial bakeries must adhere to specific equipment and sanitation requirements, cottage food operations have their own set of regulations.

All cottage foods are subject to state-specific regulations, typically focusing on shelf-stable products that don't need refrigeration making this an excellent fit for cakes, treats and baked goods. In order to prevent cottage bakers from becoming large-scale operations and bypassing retail bakery regulations, cottage bakeries often have imposed sales limitations. Additionally, there are restrictions on who cottage bakeries can market too, typically ensuring that they market exclusively using direct-to-consumer sales. This means selling to establishments like local grocery stores or bakeries is generally not allowed.

Start the process of researching your home bakery by examining the regulations applicable in your locality. Seek guidance from your state and local health departments, as they can provide you with additional information regarding the cottage food laws for home bakeries specific to your area.

Setting up your business entity

Before starting your home bakery business it's advisable to establish a business entity, such as a limited liability company (LLC). Opting for a formal company structure, as opposed to operating as an individual or sole proprietor, can safeguard your personal assets from legal liability in case of a lawsuit. Additionally, securing an insurance policy may be necessary. Consult a cottage food expert, attorney as well as an accountant to determine the most suitable course of action for your situation.

What is a business entity?

A business entity is an organization that has been formed to conduct business activities. The type of business entity is crucial because it will determine how it is taxed and who will be responsible for paying its debts and obligations.

Types of business entities

Most businesses are formed as sole proprietorships, partnerships, limited liability companies, or corporations. Which business entity is best for your home bakery? As a new home bakery business the best entity to form is a limited liability company. As your home bakery grows and scales the business entity should be changed to an S Corporation. However, it's still necessary to maintain your account or seek legal advice.

Insurance

What Is Bakers Insurance?

Bakers insurance is a liability insurance policy that has been designed to protect bakers from the cost of claims. As a baker whether you bake from home or work from a commercial kitchen space, your business faces risks that require coverage. Just one liability claim could cost your bakery thousands of dollars and damage your business reputation. Insurance can protect your business and reduce the out-of-pocket cost you may be required to pay for claims. I have always been grateful to have insurance for my cake business especially when my business feels under attack. A few years ago we created a "She's ready to pop" themed Babyshower cake. It was 3 tiers tall and very detailed. The clients opted to pick up instead of having the cake delivered. 45 min after pick up my phone rang. The cake had been set in place at the venue and left unattended and somehow fell over. "Can you fix it?" she asked. "No I'm sorry it's not possible to fix or recreate this close to the start of the event. I replied. I followed up with a number of questions like; Was the table uneven? Were there kids playing at the venue space? Did anyone accidentally bump into the cake table? The response to all of them was "No!". It would be years before she admitted that there were indeed children playing in the space and that they must have knocked the cake over. While this specific instance didn't end in legal action it brought me peace of mind to know my business was covered.

Some of the most common liability claims faced by bakers include third party bodily injury, for example a customer trips and falls in your bakery causing bodily harm, stolen or damaged equipment, or a customer gets a foodborne illness from your baked goods.

Many venues now require a COI (Certificate of Insurance) from your insurance company in order to deliver your bakery products, for example wedding cakes to their event space.

Some of the companies that provide insurance for home based bakeries

- Liberty mutual
- Simply Business
- CoverWallet
- Hiscox
- THREE
- Thimble
- Insureon

How can I get home bakery insurance?

In order to get home bakery insurance you need to have some basic information about your company on hand. The application will ask for basic facts about your business, such as your revenue and number of employees. It's as simple as completing an online application, comparing insurance quotes and choosing the best policy for your business.

Get Licensed

Before picking up your favorite spatula and starting your home baking business, it's essential to take into account additional legal considerations. Certain states may mandate a business license for the operation of a home bakery, and depending on your location, a food manager license from the health department may also be necessary.

Financial organization and creating a tax plan

Bank accounts needed

For both tax and business purposes it is vital to separate your personal and business accounts.

Because of this you need at least a business bank account and a personal bank account.

You might also be required to charge sales tax and/or food tax on the home bakery items you sell. Maintaining meticulous records of your sales, including detailed breakdowns, is essential to ensure accurate payment of the appropriate local and state taxes.

What's needed for a business bank account?

- Tax Identification Number. This is your Employer Identification Number (EIN) or a Social Security number, if you're a sole proprietorship.
- Business's formation documents. Articles of Incorporation or corporations or Articles of Organization for LLCs. Requirements may vary depending on state regulators
- Personal identification. Two forms of ID, at least one that's government issued.
- Initial deposit
- Business license.

Plan your home bakery menu

Once you have an understanding of the rules and regulations of your locality and have your business established, you can get back to the fun part of running a home bakery business, planning the menu. Most home-based bakeries create cookies, breads, muffins, cupcakes, cakes and treats. One of the biggest advantages of being your own boss allows you the freedom to craft whatever delights you want to.

Ensure that your menu aligns with local laws, keeping in mind that, in most cases, the final product must be shelf-stable, ruling out options that require refrigeration for example cream cheese.

I consider the flexibility of a home bakery to be one of its greatest advantages. You can choose to adhere to a fixed menu or implement monthly or seasonal changes, owning a home bakery allows you to adjust your offerings based on customer feedback and preferences. You can experiment with different ingredients and flavor profiles. Opting to make more of certain products during its busy seasons or scale back during slower periods.

If you're unsure about what to bake, start with baking the items you and your family love most, tweak your recipes based on feedback until it's ready to offer to the public. Constant experimentation will allow you to become familiar and master a variety of baked goods.

Purchase your equipment and supplies

After determining your Home bakery menu, it is necessary to ensure that you have all the necessary tools to bring your cakes, treats and baked creations to life. This may include assorted cake or cupcake pans, cupcake wrappers, piping bags, and tips, standing mixers, mixing bowls, scales, measuring spoons and so much more. Be proactive in preparing and organizing your supplies, ensuring you have a designated space for storage.

Certain states' cottage food laws may require that you have house your bakery equipment separate from your personal kitchen equipment, so take that into account when considering any additional space requirements. Keep a meticulous record of the costs associated with your supplies, allowing you to factor them into your menu pricing and tax calculations.

Pricing for profitability

Determining the pricing for your baked goods involves more than merely matching your competitors' rates. Think about it, what does their pricing method entail? Have they also matched the pricing of someone else? How does your business differ from theirs? Your pricing should encompass not only the costs of ingredients, labor, and additional overhead such as business fees, labor and delivery but also allow for a profit. However, figuring out the precise numbers for each element can be a complex and time consuming task. How can you navigate this calculation process effectively?

In order to properly price your cakes and baked goods there are some elements that you should ensure are covered.

- The cost of ingredients (everything from making the cakes to filling, buttercream and decor) this is the cost of creating the product
- The cost of supplies
- The cost of time/wage
- Cost of equipment
- Cost of overhead (these expenses are fixed and exist whether or not you make a cake)
- Delivery cost
- Adding a markup (this is the profit your business needs in order to grow)
- Processing fees and taxes (Typically added during invoicing) (every CRM (client management system) has a per transaction fee. If you don't include this cost into your price it will be taken out of your profit

Building out your pricing program will require some time. Take your time, this is the most taxing part of the pricing system. Remember once this information is imputed into your system, calculating your pricing becomes easier not to mention accurate.

One of the major advantages of having a system is that you will be able to determine a base price for your products. This is the cost of your cakes before customization and added elements. This base price helps you and your customers understand the minimum or starting price to do business with you and your bakery. This amount can be added to your website and posted to your social media.

The elements of a price

Let's take a closer look at each element that you should be including when costing your cakes, treats and baked goods.

Ingredients - this is the cost of everything edible that goes into making your cakes and baked goods. Cakes, fillings, buttercreams, fondant, decorations. Every single thing.

Supplies - these are the non edible elements needed to complete your orders. We break these into the following segments:

- Cake supplies - these supplies are involved in the creation of the cake but the quantity is not easily calculated. Example, parchment paper, piping bags, plastic wrap, cooking spray, skewers. For this segment we add a percentage of the total to our cake price.
- Cake decorating supplies - these are everything that is used to create your cake. Example cake boards, dowels, cake drums (100 percent of these cost will be added to your cake order).
- Cake packaging supplies - that's everything that's needed to package the cake. Cake boxes, labels (100 percent of these cost will be added to your cake order).
- Cleaning supplies - cleaning supplies are also multiple use items in your bakery that (a percentage of your cleaning supplies will be added to each order)
- Equipment - these are all the multiple use machinery and equipment needed to create our baked goods. (we add a percentage of this amount to each order)
- Overhead - these are monthly fixed costs that allow your business to run but is not directly involved in creating your cakes or baked goods. Example, rent, electricity, water, CRM, canva, website hosting, accounting, banking fees, other subscription tools (the amount will be totaled and divided by the number of cakes you make per month then added to each cake order ton account for the cost)
- Time/Wage - one of the most overlooked aspects of pricing for home bakers is charging for labor. Set a timer while doing each task involved in completing an order and log the time in a spreadsheet or notebook. Total the time it takes you to complete the order then multiply it by your hourly wage. This will vary based on wages in your area or on just

how much you want to pay yourself or finally your level of skill. Examples of tasks, mixing, decorating, shopping, sketching, client communication, etc.

- Delivery cost - delivery is priced round trip. This means the total number of miles it takes to go to and from your delivery destination. You also need to know the price per gallon of gas and how many miles your particular vehicle runs on each gallon. For example, if gas is $5 per gallon and runs 30 miles per gallon. $5 divided 30 miles is $0.17 cents per mile. If the round trip is 60 miles then multiply 60 by $0.17 giving you a round trip cost of $10.20 cents. You also need to account for the time it takes you to deliver and set up, the number of people required, toll and parking if it applies. (100 percent of the delivery fee is applied to your order)

- Markup or profit - this is typically a percentage of the total cost of your cake and it's another overlooked aspect of pricing for most home bakers. Adding a markup to your cakes and baked goods allows you to save and grow your business. It covers everything from the cost of relocating to a storefront to achieving financial freedom. Making this one of the most important aspects of pricing your cakes and baked goods

- Processing fees and taxes - Every CRM client management software charges a per transaction fee for processing the payments made to your business. If this cost is not included in the cost of the order then it will be deducted from your profit. Taxes vary from state to state but if this amount is not accounted for and saved then you will be responsible for the payments during tax season

Now that you have laid all the groundwork and you have a business entity, insurance and you are licensed. You have chosen a niche and you have gone over your numbers and priced you baked goods correctly;

Time to Open

Prepare a cross section of your menu items, arrange them attractively, and embark on your selling journey, by taking nice, clean pictures for the business social media pages, websites and portfolio. Many home bakers also sell their baked goods at farmers markets. When deciding if this avenue is a good fit for your home bakery It's crucial to research and consult local and state regulations. After you have completed all of these steps you are well on your way to having a successful home bakery business

CHAPTER 4: MARKETING AND BRANDING YOUR BAKING BUSINESS

Tips and strategies for marketing and branding, including social media, online marketing, and branding strategies.

Steps to create a strong brand

- What defines a bakery brand?

A brand represents the unique identity and narrative of a bakery business, distinguishing it from competitors offering similar products, services and baked goods. The objective of branding is to carve a distinctive space in the minds of the target audience, positioning the bakery as their preferred choice for purchasing their baked foods.

- What is branding in your bakery business?

Branding is the creation of a bakery's brand identity, including elements such as a logo, tagline, visual design, and tone of voice.

In essence, branding is the entire procedure of researching, developing, and implementing distinctive features that characterize your bakery. This approach enables consumers to associate your brand with the products or services you offer.

The impact of branding your bakery extends to various aspects, from social media captions to color palettes and packaging materials. Bakeries adept at building strong brands understand that their brand identity should permeate every aspect of their presence. Recognizing that their bakery name goes beyond mere labels, they strategically employ branding to captivate consumers and stand out in a crowded market.

- What's the difference in branding vs marketing a bakery business?

Although it may seem simple to combine branding and marketing into a single entity, there are distinct differences. Comparisons between branding and marketing often involve discussions about their respective priorities. The reality is that both are integral to the success of a business and must align effectively for sustained growth of your bakery business.

In essence, branding makes up the identity of a bakery, while marketing covers the tactics and strategies employed to communicate that vision to the world.

Importance of branding in business

- What is the importance of branding your bakery business?

Undoubtedly, your brand stands as one of your bakery's most important assets. It not only provides identity but also ensures memorability, fosters consumer trust, amplifies the effectiveness of your marketing and advertising efforts, and instills a sense of pride among your employees.

Additional advantages of branding your bakery include, Influencing purchase decisions. Branding can serve as the decisive factor for consumers when deciding which bakery to buy from.

Establishing Business Identity. A brand extends beyond a bakery's product or service, providing a distinct identity. Branding offers consumers something to relate to and connect with beyond the specific product or service being purchased.

Enhancing Memorability. Branding makes your bakery business memorable, serving as the face of your bakery. It aids consumers in distinguishing your bakery business from others in your industry.

Amplifying Advertising and Marketing. Branding supports your marketing and advertising endeavors, giving your promotional efforts added impact and recognition.

Steps to create a strong brand

Determine your ideal client avatar target audience

Branding is the catalyst for awareness, recognition, trust, and eventually revenue in your bakery business. However, in order to get these outcomes you need the right consumers. And not just any consumers, your ideal client or specific target audience and customers. Most customers want to have a memorable experience in order to purchase from your bakery business. But how can you deliver such an experience without a clear understanding of who they are?

If your bakery brand fails to resonate with your audience, achieving awareness, recognition, trust, and revenue becomes problematic. This is where targeted market research plays a crucial role.

Before getting started, it's imperative to understand the people your branding aims to attract. Who is the intended recipient of your product, service or baked goods? Who constitutes your ideal customer? What motivated the creation of your business?

Insights gained from your target market research and the development of buyer personas will significantly influence your subsequent branding decisions. Therefore, prioritize this initial step as it sets the foundation for your branding journey.

The following questions will help you determine your ideal client avatar or target audience.

An ideal client avatar is a profile that lays out a set of principles and characteristics that describes the ideal person who would purchase your product, service or baked goods. Your avatar is the ideal person that you want to sell or market your products to.

Let's start with your price point - Calculate your base cost to do business with your bakery by taking into account all the elements that need to be included when costing your cake and baked goods, ingredients, supplies, equipment, overhead, time/labor cost as well as your desired profit margin and use that information to determine your starting price point. What is that number for your business?

Is your ideal client male or female - Who would be most attracted to the type of cake designs that you want to create?

What age group do they fall in? - For example 25-34, 35-44, 45-54, 55-64

Is your ideal client married or single? - are they the decision maker or do they need to discuss things with a partner? Who is responsible for the final buying decision?

Is your ideal client employed or unemployed? - I imagine that it would be hard for an unemployed customer to buy from your bakery or pay a premium price for your product, service or baked goods.

What is their average income?- based on your pricing how much would that person make weekly, monthly or yearly in order to afford your cakes?

Where does that person live? - based on your pricing, where can that person afford to live? (In your neighborhood or a different neighborhood). Do they rent or own their home?

Where do they shop? - are they more health conscious and shops at Trader Joes or are they looking for a bargain, stocks up in bulk from BJ's, Target or Walmart? Macys or Saks?

Do they drive or take public transportation? - If your ideal customer drives it becomes easier for them to travel to your bakery location.

Do they have children?- Customers who are parents often have more budget constraints than those who don't.

Being a good cake designer alone will not get you business, people will want to know you and like you, as a person, so who is the woman/person behind the baker? Who are you really?

Brand identity

Your brand identity reflects how you wish your brand to be recognized. Essentially, you need to pinpoint both your personal "why" and the "why" of your business. What motivated the establishment of your home bakery? Does it address a specific problem or fulfill a gap in your local community or market? Understanding your brand identity is essential. Without clarity on this aspect, it becomes challenging to convey its necessity to the buying public and cultivate brand awareness.

When building a brand identity it's important to do the following:

Identify your mission: why did you start your bakery business? Providing an answer to this question is instrumental in shaping your mission statement. This statement communicates the purpose and passion that define your bakery.

What are the goals of your business? In today's social media age people want to get to know you, and your business. They want to be taken on a journey through your ups and downs. They want to root for you and your business.

To construct a bakery brand that resonates with your audience, garners value, and instills trust, you must effectively convey what your bakery brings to the table. Subsequently, every facet of your brand—be it the logo, tagline, imagery, voice, or personality—can authentically reflect that mission and vision.

Consider your mission statement as a foundational element of your brand manifesto, encapsulating the essence of why your organization exists and compelling people to care about your brand.

Why did I start my business?

Honestly, at that juncture, my passion for cake decorating was so all-encompassing that it felt more like an inevitability than a conscious choice. It occupied every waking hour of my life. I devoured every cake decorating video on YouTube and Google, even though the content available was limited at the time. I amassed a collection of tools, equipment, and an abundance of cutters—so many cutters. It took several years before I even contemplated the mission of my business.

Our mission is to help every client design their dream wedding/event cake. To produce products that not only look phenomenal but taste just as good. We do this by using the highest quality bakery products and providing the best possible service to our clients. We will cautiously improve all aspects of our business to sustain the long-term success of our business and to provide exceptional customer service to our clients.

Establish your unique value proposition: your company's unique value is what sets it apart from the competition. What makes it different? It is a statement that tells your customers how your offer will benefit them and explains what makes it distinctive. This is so important that once you determine your unique value proposition every ad or advertising campaign you run for your bakery business should align with its messaging.

VALUE STATEMENT/GUIDING PRINCIPLES

HONESTY - Never encourage clients to spend more than they can afford.

QUALITY - Always use the highest quality ingredients.

LISTEN - Listen to my clients, take their many ideas and incorporate them into an inclusive   design.

TREND -   Be knowledgeable about changing trends in the wedding/event cake industry, while not losing sight of my clients love story.

INVEST -   Invest in myself as well as in new products on a continual basis to maintain our competitiveness in today's market.

CULTIVATE -   A following of people that buys our products and contributes to our success.

Listen, highly custom wedding cakes are not a necessity, it's a luxury. It's a want not a need. I work closely with clients' budgets in order to create maximum impact but I am not the cheap cake lady. I will never push clients out of their financial comfort zone when designing for them but it's imperative that clients understand that my cakes are a luxury item.

Create your brand's visual identity: By now, you should have a grasp of your target audience, your mission statement, and the distinctive qualities defining your bakery business.

If you can confidently complete these steps, it's time to move on to one of the more exhilarating aspects of branding—the visual design. This encompasses elements like your logo, color palette, typography (fonts), and other visual components. This is most people's idea of what branding is. The part that is shown to the public. That they recognize and associate with your company. They all combine to set a mood and tone for your business.

Here's a real-life anecdote: a few years back, my fiancée Fabian surprised me with a new logo. He organized a competition, we selected a design, suggested tweaks, and the entire process was amazing. However, when it came time to provide the final colors, I found myself clueless about where to begin in choosing them. In the end, I went with the colors suggested by the designer. It turned out that the colors representing my company, the ones the world associates with my brand, was not a decision I made based on my own understanding of myself and my business. Back then, I lacked knowledge about color palettes, color choices, and their meanings. Reflecting on this experience, it's crucial to consider what truly matters when developing your branding.

Increase brand recognition: if you build it they will come. Well unfortunately it takes time to get the buying public to associate your company with your branding. To help this process along generate awareness through your website, social media and advertising platforms. Create marketing campaigns. Ensure that your messaging, mission, unique value proposition and visual identity is consistent across all platforms.

The importance of consistency in branding, messaging and your work across all platforms is vital. Clients needs to understand exactly the level of skill and service they will get while working with you and your business

Brand Image

Your brand image is similar to your brand identity in that it deals with how your brand is known. Your brand identity is how you want your brand to be known whereas your brand image is how your brand is actually known. This is the reputation that your home baker currently has with the buying public. For example if you're building your brand identity as unique custom cakes and treats, a company that utilized all gourmet, organic products but the buying public views your business as cheap but delicious. The cake lady that would take their last min orders, at a lower price and produce a replica product. Some ways that you can establish and maintain a strong and positive brand image are:

Create a schedule that allows you to finish your orders before pickup so that you can get pictures. Invest in lighting and do at least a few basic edits before posting your pics and BTS photos and videos. Show your process and progress but keep it consistent.

Use PR to spread your home bakeries messaging: this can be done through news outlets, blog posts and influencer posts. Public relations will help your home bakery raise awareness of your brand and help to improve your brand image.

Do a bit of research, reach out to influencers in your niche, put your business out there. You can build it but they won't come to you if they don't know you exist.

Establish a social media presence: the world today is very much driven by social media making it one of the most effective ways to build a brand image. You can do this by sharing content with potential customers, keeping them up to date on new bakery products and flavors, engaging with potential customers and it can also be used as a way to address negative feedback. Show your customers that you care and are taking steps to address their issues.

Share your journey, the good, the bad, the ugly. Example recipes you might be working to perfect. When it's going well and when it's not. What tweaks did you make? What changed for them last time you tried.

Create quality content: posting content relevant to your home bakery and brand increases both awareness and web traffic to your business. This also helps you to build authority in the industry. By posting content that educates your buying public you will become a trusted source of information which will help improve your brands reputation and trust.

If you want to make kids cakes you can write captions or create posts explaining to parents the best cake and filling combinations for school birthday parties. Educate on the importance of being aware of allergens. Why harsh colors may be pretty but turn their kids mouths into unflattering colors.

Brand Culture

Brand culture refers to your company's core values and the example you set portraying them.

While companies have always stated values like "honesty" and "reliability" in recent years there has been a shift towards moral stances. These types of values feed into and help you build your brand's culture. A few ways that you can build brand culture are:

Your values: define your values and show clear examples of how you and your company live them in today's society. Don't be afraid to take a stance, remember you can't please everyone.

While my cakes are a luxury item it's one of my core values to work within my clients budgets (reasonably of course) I solve problems by suggesting for instance that they order a smaller fully custom cake and add sheet cakes to cover the guest count. By being upfront and making it known that not everyone eats cake and suggesting 60-75% of the guest could be enough servings. This information can be found across my social platforms, website and through conversions with me. This makes me trustworthy and clients are willing to spend more where trust exists.

Spread awareness of your values: let customers know about your values by talking about them on social media and listing them on your website. Encourage discussions and build community around them.

Let them know that you're human and willing to talk about the hard stuff.

Ensure that your company reflects your values: it's not enough to just list a few cherry picked values because they look good on your website and social media. Choose values that you live daily thereby making it easy to show real life examples. There is nothing people love to hate more than a hypocrite.

Do not fake this. Add them as they become clear to you. Be true to yourself and your business and the public will recognise that you are authentic

Brand Personality

Your brand personality refers to the human traits that your home based bakery has. Creating a brand personality is imperative in order to connect with potential customers on an emotional level. This helps make your brand relatable to your buying public. A few ways that create a brand personality are:

Learn and understand your audience: learning your audience is an integral step and should be done from the very beginning. How you communicate, how you present yourself and your home bakery should reflect not just who your audience is but what they expect. (you don't for instance want to be talking to brides or couples when your audience 90 moms and parents looking for birthday cakes)

Engage with your audience: while written captions are important and help you get your point across, lives and videos converts better when trying to engage with your audience.

Be consistent in tone: be authentic with yourself and your buying public. If you're funny, be funny across your website and all your social media platforms. This tone should be the same in person and online so that your authenticity can carry over. You don't want to play a part/role with your buying public. Be yourself, they will love you.

How to stand out in the baking industry

My number one biggest piece of advice on standing out in the baking industry is taste. It comes first, last and always. Even in today's market where cakes, pastries and baking has been made popular by tv, social media and streaming services the number one comment i receive during consultations is "I went to ____ wedding and the cake was beautiful, but it tasted like cardboard"

Learn your recipes, test, tweak, understand how the ingredients work together. When you can bake them with consistency across all sizes then and only then should they be added to your menu.

Consistency: be consistent in taste, texture and moisture levels. The taste of your bakery products at the tasting should be the same at the wedding and the follow up anniversary. It should be able to spark a memory.

Customer service: treat your customers well. They are living breathing people with lives and problems that need solving, they're not just your next rent payment. Solve their problems, listen and take into account their feelings. If you do this you will gain not just lifetime customers but raving fans.

Create work that you're proud of: at the end of the day everything that walks out the door bears your name whether or not you laid a finger on it. Be proud of what you produce. Take your time, practice, and work diligently to improve your business and skill.

What is a niched cake business?

A niche bakery serves a specific type of baked goods and targets a very specific customer base. Choosing to niche your cake business makes your bakery products highly sought after for its uniqueness.

Example - I chose to niche as a wedding cake designer with a specialty in sugar flowers.

Why - After 14 years in the baking industry and making cakes across the board it was the area that I gravitated to the most. While I didn't mind the countless hours spent making detailed pieces for kids' cakes, I just love the conversions I get to have with couples looking to book their dream wedding cake. Even the ones on the fence. Just getting a feel for the person in the room that most needs my attention and making them feel seen and heard while still including their partner. I just love it.

Is choosing a niche helpful? How

It is a common misconception to think that if your bakery has a wide variety of products, designs or styles that it will appeal to more customers. For most cake businesses the opposite is actually true. By limiting your product range or your target market you will find it easier to grow your cake business.

Nicheing your home bakery business can be helpful in the following ways:

By picking the right niche, for instance where there isn't much competition you will find it easier to get your bakery noticed by customers.

Consistently over deliver - this will make you the go to person for cakes in your specific niche and you will basically own that space/niche.

By niching - It's easier to target your market as it's smaller and more clearly defined.

By combining niching and over-delivery you can easily create loyal fans that will happily rave about you and your products to others.

Example: I chose a niche as a cake designer that specializes in sugar flowers.

Why: Two years ago I developed such a love of all things sugar flowers. Prior to that it was a struggle to make, shape, dust, it was nightmarish. Then I found the right class and the right instructor and boy now it's simply amazing. To make them and bring them to life. Can you tell I just love it?

How to choose a cake business niche?

As most bakers that aren't niched would tell you after months or years of caking, certain events or types of cake design become favorites to create. For me that became wedding cakes. I love every aspect from designing with couples, baking, making decor elements and watching it all come together. Finding the segment of the baking industry that fits you best can be tricky. If you're looking to niche your home bakery business you need to do the following:

Research your niche market - gather as much information as possible about this area. What products are doing well and what isn't. Is there a way that you can make certain products better or a particular problem in that area that you can solve.

What are your passions and interests - is there an area in the bakery industry that you just love. That you do just for fun, in your free time and you just can't stop learning about it? For me, that's my love of sugar flowers.

Identify a problem that you can solve - as business owners one of our main goals is to solve our clients problems. Take the time to think and brainstorm about it. Is there a problem that you have solved for yourself or your clients that others would benefit from?

Example: for me one of the biggest ways that i solve my clients problem is by taking their married cake designs ideas and combining them into one cohesive design, sprinkling it with fairy dust and helping them create their dream wedding cake

Example: Kate's son has a gluten allergy and none of the bakeries in her area offered gluten free cakes or baked goods. She had to travel two towns over in order to purchase his birthday cake. The cake turned out to be dry and tasteless. Kate started researching and tweaking gluten free recipes in a quest to make her family cakes and baked goods that they could actually enjoy. After months of trial and error Kate had a few base recipes that her family loved. The time she spent baking and decorating gluten free cakes she developed a love for all things cake decorating. She wondered if other moms in her area had a similar problem so she did some research and decided to start a Gluten free cake business to service her neighborhood.

Experiment - if you're passionate about more than one area of the baking industry then try out each segment until you find the best fit for you and your home bakery business.

Example: for some of you, you already know how you would like to niche. For me it took 14 years before I realized that hey I don't want to make every type of cake. I want to really focus on weddings and couples. Do i still make cakes outside of my niche yes all the time however its not the focus of my advertising, its rarely posted to my A's Exquisite Cakes page. Why do I still make cakes outside of my niche? Over the past 16 years in business I have built relationships with people, families and I took the time to foster them and now it's hard to move completely away, not to mention the new relationships that I am building with current wedding cake clients. They will also turn into future orders.

Feedback - discuss your options with those who can be trusted to give their honest opinions. Take your feelings out of it and focus on the issue at hand, finding the right niche for you and your business.

Keywords here (trusted opinions only) not people who will put your down and doubt your choices and career path

Research the competition - A mentor once told me " There is nothing new under the sun" if you're thinking of doing it chances are it's been done before. Research similar business. What's working for them and what isn't. What's their pricing structure? Take note of their branding and content strategy but I caution you to still keep your work original to you and your business.

I want you to truly understand that the goal is not to copy but to understand the person's business model. If you can add a similar product the by all means do so but don't just recreate

Is it profitable? - I understand that when choosing a niche this may not be an immediate focus for you but if you're going to build and grow a sustainable business it needs to be able not only make money but be profitable.

Examples of niches in the cake industry:

- Gravity defying cakes
- Wedding cakes
- Birthday or celebration cakes
- Hyper realistic cakes
- Cookies
- Treat tables
- Cupcakes

Other ways that you can niche in the baking industry:

Niche by what you bake

One of the ways that you can niche is by considering what you bake in your bakery. Do you have specific knowledge or insight into a specific area? Example: dairy free or vegan, egg free, exotic flavor combinations, boozy cakes and cupcakes.

Niche by the type of baked good or event you love the most.

If you're like me then you may have a niche in pineapple tarts and wedding cakes lol but seriously. Is there a baked good that you're obsessed with baking? This could be your niche!

Marketing strategies for bakeries

Tips for utilizing social media and online platforms

Learn How to use Instagram

Start with Reels

What to use them for - trends, behind the scenes, storytelling, engagement

Carousels

What to use them for - How to's, tutorials, case studies, photo dumps.

Single image

What to use them for - good captions, infographics, tweets/memes, about you.

Stories

What to use them for - personal, engagement boost, community based, promotional

CHAPTER 5: BUILDING CUSTOMER RELATIONSHIPS

Advice on how to build strong relationships with customers to ensure repeat business and word-of-mouth referrals

What are customer relationships in the bakery business?

Successful bakeries thrive on strong customer relationships, serving as one of the most important links between your bakery brand and its customers. These relationships encompass the entire history of interactions between your bakery business and customers, laying the groundwork for future transactions. The quality of past interactions with customers often influences the likelihood of future engagements or purchases.

During periods of market and economic uncertainty, the importance of establishing and nurturing positive customer relationships becomes even more apparent. Acquiring new customers becomes more challenging, prompting a shift in focus towards the need to retain existing ones.

Good customer relationships are characterized by a back and forth communication approach, leading to elevated customer satisfaction. Interactions that not only meet but surpass customer expectations, fosters loyalty and encourages repeat purchases. By providing consistent customer experience, the overall lifetime value of your audience improves. Customers become passionate about acquiring your products and services because they feel valued and heard.

Why are customer relationships important to your bakery business?

The success of your bakery depends on its customer relationships. The greater your investment in fostering connections between your bakery and customers, the greater the possibility it becomes to realize returns on investment across various aspects of your bakery business.

For instance, dedicating resources to enhance customer relationships may yield:

Enhanced Customer Loyalty:

Implementing robust customer relationships helps to cultivate loyalty, prompting customers to choose your bakery over others in your community consistently. Building loyal customer relationships is a slow process that requires multiple positive experiences between your bakery and customers. Investing in customer experiences speeds up the development of lasting relationships, enabling a quicker conversion of your audience into a loyal following. Every interaction should reinforce the belief that your brand is worth returning to. Whether through exceptional customer service, a well-crafted loyalty program, or the establishment of a personal connection, customers who perceive a trustworthy relationship with your brand are more likely to become not just loyal patrons but raving fans.

Increase customer retention:

Consistent experiences nurtured in customer-brand relationships contribute to lower customer loss rates. Building strong relationships with customers ensures that they know what to expect when doing business with your bakery. This assures your customers that each interaction with your bakery will deliver consistently exceptional experience or service.

Higher Customer Lifetime Value (CLV):

Loyal customers, returning to your bakery because of the personal connections you've established, contribute to an increased Customer Lifetime Value. With each return visit, they not only offer more value but also incur lower costs for your bakery business.

Lower Customer Acquisition Costs:

Investing in relationships proves to be a cost-effective strategy, as existing customers exhibit a 60 to 70% likelihood of making a purchase compared to the lower 5% to 20% probability with new leads. Moreover, acquiring a new customer can be up to five times more expensive than retaining an existing one. By prioritizing customer satisfaction, you reduce the need for extensive outreach efforts, as satisfied customers are more inclined to recommend your bakery, organically bringing in new customers as the referral comes not from the bakery itself but a trusted source.

Strategies for building strong relationships

Five steps to building better customer relationships

Regardless of whether you're a small home bakery or a franchise, the success of your business is likely to be shaped by your interactions with customers. To guide you in establishing lasting customer relationships, I've outlined five steps for improving customer relationships. Customers who invest time in providing feedback are seeking a mutually beneficial relationship with your bakery, offering valuable insights for future interactions to strengthen these connections.

However, it's important to understand that once customers provide feedback they are looking for your bakery to act on them, failing to acknowledge or respond to customer feedback, or neglecting to demonstrate its incorporation, can lead to waning interest. Strong customer/bakery relationship can withstand constructive criticism, and ultimately, your customers are the ones you aim to impress. Consider instead letting your customers know when you've heeded their feedback, fostering a two-way customer relationship based on mutual understanding. Expressing gratitude to customers who share feedback and providing incentives to encourage others to contribute their perspectives for example a percentage off their next order.

1. Establish Effective Communication:

Consistent and thoughtful communication, whether through newsletters, follow-up phone calls, or the occasional check-in text messages, is essential for reaching customers and forging enduring connections.

2. Ask for and Act on Customer Feedback:

It's worth mentioning again that maintaining an open line of communication for clients to provide suggestions on improvements is crucial for customer satisfaction. Requesting feedback through surveys or other outreach methods demonstrates a commitment to enhancing the customer experience. Check your ego at the bakery doors and get to work improving your cakes, treats, baked goods and service based on the customer feedback received.

3. Cultivate Trust:

In your home bakery business trust forms the bedrock of a successful working blaker/customer relationship. Consistently delivering quality, timeliness, and reliability is vital. In cases where expectations are not met, provide a transparent explanation of what transpired, and outline the steps being taken to prevent a recurrence.

4. Humanize Interactions:

Customers are human beings who appreciate being treated with respect and kindness. Always remember that there is a person on the other end of every phone call or email, and acknowledge their humanity in your interactions.

5. Reward Loyalty:

Implement incentives, such as discounts for repeat customers or VIP customer rewards programs, to solidify long-term customer loyalty. Regularly express appreciation to customers, conveying that their loyalty is valued and recognized.

Tips for handling customer complaints

1. Remain Emotionally Neutral

Whether it's a well-meaning individual offering constructive feedback or a dissatisfied customer yelling in frustration, it's crucial to approach any customer complaint without letting personal emotions interfere. Maintain composure, attentively listen to their concerns, and respond calmly.

2. Refrain from Contesting Their Grievance

It's a natural instinct to want to correct a customer when their complaint seems to be invalid. However, challenging their perspective can escalate the situation. Instead of refuting their concerns, focus instead on actively listening to their feedback. Consider expressing gratitude by thanking them for their input, this unexpected tactic might yield surprising benefits.

3. Acknowledge Their Concerns

While listening to customer complaints is not the most pleasant task, make a concerted effort to genuinely understand the nature of their concerns.

Whether it's dissatisfaction with delayed service, the wrong flavor cake, or encounters with yourself or specific employees, acknowledge the specifics of their complaint. Confirm that you understand their message, reinforcing the importance of their perspective.

4. Provide Support

Support can take various forms, ranging from active listening to practical solutions such as placing a new order for cakes and treats or discount off a future order. The nature of your support should be tailored to the specifics of the customer's complaint. Having actively listened, you should be equipped to suggest several ways to address their concerns, or ideally, propose a well-defined and optimal solution. Your judgment comes into play here, considering what would work best. Remember, effective support entails offering the customer something in response to their complaint. It's worth noting that if your initial offering falls short of their expectations, persistence is key, it will be worth it to your bakeries reputation to offer more or a larger discount that to deal with a negative review or a customer speaking ill about your bakery to others.

5. Demonstrate Flexibility

In the hopefully rear cases where a satisfactory resolution seems elusive, consider alternative ways to assist your customer. For instance, implementing a bakery policy of offering $20 gift cards to a local flower shop for upset customers can be a creative and thoughtful gesture. An additional tip is to negotiate with the flower shop for complimentary or discounted cards, fostering mutually beneficial network marketing benefiting both businesses. In such instances, thinking outside the box and displaying flexibility is paramount.

6. Confirm Understanding

After suggesting a resolution or making clear the extent of your assistance in response to their complaint, gently inquire if the customer understands the steps you're willing to take. Make sure to do this respectfully, conveying your intention. Simply put, ask the customer if they have grasped how you will address their concerns or, conversely, if you cannot fulfill additional requests.

7. Apologize with Gratitude

The phrase "I'm sorry" can sometimes ring hollow, and sincerity is crucial especially when dealing with an aggrieved customer. Aim to genuinely convey your apology while expressing appreciation for the customer. Communicate regret for any inconvenience, disappointment, or distress they experienced, coupled with gratitude for the opportunity to address the issue together. This authentic effort often resonates positively, leaving a lasting impression even if complete satisfaction is not immediate.

8. Follow-Up

After extending your apology, demonstrating gratitude, and providing support, explore additional ways to assist customers who have voiced complaints. One effective approach is to follow up within 24 to 48 hours, this needs to be done by you, the owner, not an employee of your bakery. This demonstrates ongoing care and shows that their concerns remain a priority for you and your bakery, this step reinforces your commitment to customer satisfaction.

9. Move Forward

Believe it or not for most home bakers this will be the hardest step to take. Ultimately, dwelling on customer complaints can impede progress. While occasional complaints are inevitable, home bakers must have a strategic plan to navigate these situations seamlessly, professionally, and gracefully. Moving forward allows you to focus on the next tasks at hand (literally your next order). Businesses that effectively manage complaints not only retain customers willing to give them another chance but also benefit from positive word-of-mouth marketing from satisfied customers. This timeless approach to customer care never goes out of style.

Advice for encouraging repeat business

8 Strategies for encouraging repeat business in your home bakery

1. Implement a Subscription Model:

Explore the rising trend of subscription-based businesses by offering monthly subscriptions like "cake of the month club". Recurring billing ensures a steady stream of repeat orders.

2. Launch a Loyalty Program:

Encourage repeat purchases by rewarding your bakery's customers with loyalty points, freebies, and discounts. A well-designed loyalty program sets your brand apart, fostering customer satisfaction and retention.

3. Prioritize Excellent Customer Service:

Deliver outstanding customer service to create a positive buying experience. Leverage customer insights programs, respond to inquiries promptly. Ensure your and your staff focuses on building lasting customer relationships.

4. Harness the Power of Retargeting Ads:

Increase the likelihood of repeat purchases through retargeting ads. Strategically display engaging content to customers who have previously engaged with your business on social media. Optimize your ads by experimenting with various formats and leveraging A/B testing.

5. Invest in Personalization:

Enhance customer engagement and loyalty through personalized marketing campaigns. Divide customers based on demographics and behavior, send targeted emails, provide tailored product and service recommendations to strengthen the customer-bakery connection.

6. Offer Freebies and Discounts:

Attract and retain customers by offering appealing discounts and freebies. Consider creative incentives, such as discounts on future purchases, or the addition of treats to a future custom cake order, to give customers a reason to return to your bakery.

7. Maintain an Active Social Media Presence:

Build trust and brand loyalty through a consistent social media strategy. Create visually appealing content that resonates with your customers and actively engage with customers through comments and shares. Customers love behind the scenes footage as well as finished styled shots. Almost anything that you do in your home bakery can be recorded and shared on your bakery's social media platforms.

8. Solicit Customer Feedback:

Capture customer feedback to improve their experiences. Implement changes based on feedback to demonstrate that you value customer opinions and are committed to enhancing their experience.

By following these strategies, your home bakery business can create engaging customer experiences, fortify brand loyalty, and unlock the potential for increased repeat purchases.

CHAPTER 6: SCALING YOUR BAKING BUSINESS

Numerous home bakers start their home bakers with dreams of scaling their business and one day moving into a brick and mortar storefront space. In order to progress from harboring ambitious dreams to reality, bakers need to formulate a strategic plan to enlarge or scale the business.

Scaling a bakery business involves assessing whether there exists increased demand and profit potential in a broader market. While not all businesses are conducive to scaling, a careful examination can help determine if this strategy aligns with your bakeries objectives and pinpoint the opportune moment to embark on expansion.

Scaling vs growing. While growing a business shares similarities with scaling, the distinction lies in the cost implications of expansion. In order to scale it is necessary to have an increase in revenue without a proportional increase in expenses. On the other hand, growing entails simultaneous increases in both revenue and expenses.

Understanding the Right Time to Scale

Scaling a business is a significant step that should be taken with careful consideration. It's not merely about increasing sales; it's about sustainable growth. To determine if your business is ready to scale, consider the following indicators:

Consistent Increase in Demand: Are you consistently selling more than you can produce? Is there a steady increase in customer inquiries and orders?

Financial Stability: Do you have a stable cash flow that can support expansion?

Market Opportunity: Is there a gap in the market that your business can fill? Are there trends or customer needs that you have yet to exploit?

Capacity for Growth: Do you have the physical space, equipment, and manpower to grow?

Developing a Scaling Strategy

Once you've established the need to scale, the next step is creating a comprehensive scaling strategy. This involves:

- Market Research: Understand your current market and potential new markets. Identify customer segments and tailor your expansion to meet their needs.
- Financial Planning: Calculate the cost of expansion, including equipment, additional staff, marketing, and other overheads. Prepare a detailed financial forecast.
- Quality Control Systems: Implement systems to maintain the quality of your products as you increase production.
- Hiring and Managing Staff

Choosing the Right Location

- If expansion means moving to a new location or opening additional outlets, consider:
- Accessibility and Visibility: The new location should be easily accessible to customers and suppliers.
- Space and Layout: Ensure that the space is adequate for your production, storage, and sales needs.
- Market Research: Understand the local market and competition in the new area.
- Implementing Technology

How to scale a bakery business

When initiating the process of scaling your home bakery business, consider the following steps to stay on course:

- Assemble the right team.

Scaling your bakery invariably involves expanding your team to support larger operations. This can be achieved by hiring employees, or engaging contractors. When hiring, patience is crucial when working with individuals possessing diverse skill sets, particularly when they are new to your bakery.

- Develop a growth strategy

Create a simple and transparent strategy that can be easily understood and embraced by employees, customers, and vendors. While aiming to stand out among competitors, remain focused on your core offering, values and brand promise. Staying true to a specialized service or your bakerys niche enhances the chances of connecting with customers and successfully scaling the business.

- Formulate a game plan.

Once stakeholders are aligned and the target audience is identified, devise a plan by prioritizing tasks, determining metrics for measuring business growth, and enhancing staff meetings to keep the team informed about the scaling process.

- Secure financing

Scaling can necessitate the need for significant financial resources, and it is crucial to determine how to fund your expansion plans. While bootstrapping with personal funds offers independence and avoids external borrowing, many bakery businesses may require additional capital sources. Options include small business loans, lines of credit, or seeking equity from external investors. Carefully evaluate the costs associated with each financing option.

Is it the right time to scale?

Before deciding to scale your home bakery business, figure out your long-term goals within the bakery business plan. Understand the purpose of scaling and how it aligns with your company's objectives. Gather insights from core customers to understand their interactions with your business and identify opportunities to expand the customer base. Asking customers relevant questions helps gauge their expectations and experiences, providing valuable information for reaching new customers and starting the scaling process.

Next steps after scaling a business

After successfully scaling your home bakery business, consider assuming a new role or implementing training tools to bring staff members up to speed. Monitor accounting and financial reporting closely, recognizing the higher risk of potential challenges with more people involved in the business.

Be prepared for growing pains that may arise during scaling, such as adjustments to company culture. Employees accustomed to the startup environment may find it challenging to adapt to the structured nature of a larger company. Maintaining realistic expectations is essential, as it takes time to find stability and success as a larger operation.

Hiring and managing staff

To ensure that your baking business stands out, the recruitment and management of top-tier bakers are paramount. But where do you begin?

As a bakery owner, your goal is to hire the best bakers who can contribute to the success of your business. But how do you locate the right candidates for the job? In this section, we'll walk you through the process step by step.

Craft a job description

Understanding what's required of an employee at every position of your bakery business and developing a series of captivating job descriptions is crucial to attracting bakers to your bakery business. To ensure that your job description stands out, it should be specific and detailed, highlighting the unique features of your bakery and the expectations of every role being advertised. Make sure your job description includes the following:

- Details of the role (job title, salary, location, hours of work/shift patterns, ideal start date)
- A summary of the general responsibilities for the role
- Requirements for the role (e.g., qualifications, soft skills)
- A brief overview of your business
- A summary of any benefits (e.g., holiday allowance)
- How to apply! (e.g., Send a CV to an email address)
- Optional - Include when interviews will be starting and an outline of the process.

Some potential job roles for your bakery may include:

- Bakery managers: Overseeing the bakery's operations, managing staff, ordering supplies, setting production goals, and ensuring profitability.
- Head bakers: Managing baking operations, creating recipes, overseeing production, training staff, and ensuring the quality of baked goods.

- Pastry chefs: Creating and preparing various desserts and pastries, including cakes, cookies, and macaroons.
- Baker's assistants: Assisting the head baker in preparing and baking various baked goods, including pastries, and cakes.

When crafting your job description, include specific responsibilities, qualifications, and skills required for each role, be as detailed as possible. For example, a pastry chef may require formal culinary training, while a baker's assistant may only require home baking experience.

It's also essential to highlight any unique perks of working at your bakery, such as a friendly work environment, opportunities for professional growth, or flexible scheduling. Creating a detailed and appealing job description can attract the right candidates to your bakery and set your business up for success.

Review resumes and applications

Now that you've crafted a job description, it's time to start the process of finding the best bakery staff for your business! When reviewing resumes and applications, keep in mind the work environment you will like to build and the quality of service that you want to provide.

While it's crucial to look for candidates with the skills and experience outlined in your job description, don't hesitate to consider those with slightly less experience that may possess other qualities and express willingness to learn. The best bakers are often the ones who bring something extra to the table.

Don't discount candidates with certifications and specialized training. A candidate with a

Interview candidates

Don't be afraid to ask questions that allow candidates to showcase their skills and experience while infusing a bit of showcasing their personality. After all, the perfect candidate for each position may not just excel at baking but may bring their own special personality that will add to the working environment/community you're building.

This is your chase to provide potential employees with information about your business. Discuss your bakery's goals and values. This helps determine if the candidate aligns with your vision, mission and possesses the qualities necessary to add to the success of your bakery.

It's important to determine the level of challenges they have faced and gauge their ability to pivot and overcome challenging baking situations. This provides insight into their baking skills and ability to think on their feet.

Offer

Once you've identified the perfect baker(s) for your team, it's time to extend an offer. Offer a competitive salary and benefits package, be sure to highlight any unique perks of working at your bakery. Remember, your bakery employees are the backbone of your business, so fair compensation is essential for their hard work and dedication.

By following these steps, you'll be well on your way hiring the best bakers and building the community needed for your bakery business to be successful.

Employee management

Now that you have assembled the perfect team of bakers for your bakery it's time to effectively manage and lead them.

Creating a Positive Work Environment

It's key to understand the significance of fostering a positive work environment to retain happy and motivated employees. Whether your bakery is a bustling brick-and-mortar store or a home kitchen space, ensuring your staff feels valued and supported is crucial to your bakery's success.

Encourage employee input and collaboration to foster opportunities for growth and learning.

Recognize and reward hard work, acknowledging achievements when your employees reach or surpasses goals or goes above and beyond. Provide opportunities for rest and relaxation, such as regular breaks or occasional outings during working hours, remember that working at a bakery is a very taxing job. Be flexible, allowing employees time off, especially to address family commitments. Establish open lines of communication, displaying team goals prominently and involving all necessary personnel in decision-making.

Train your staff

No matter the position that is filled, never assume that the employee has the knowledge to start work at your bakery. Provide a comprehensive training program that teaches employees the skills they need to have to work in your bakery. If any gaps in knowledge become apparent, address it immediately. Create an employee handbook as well as systems and processes in your bakery business to ensure that it operates smoothly.

Greeting Customers with a Smile

In a bakery, your team often serves as the face of your business, interacting with customers. Encourage your staff to be friendly and approachable. Ensure all staff are well-informed about products and your business, fostering confidence in handling customer inquiries. Seek customer feedback regularly to ensure excellent service and gather insights for implementing new ideas.

Setting Goals and Expectations

To maximize your bakery's potential, set clear goals and expectations for your staff. Ensure your employees understand what is expected of them. Provide the necessary resources for your staff to succeed. Hold regular meetings inviting all staff to review progress toward business goals.

Celebrate accomplishments when goals are achieved

Providing Feedback and Recognition Offering feedback and recognition can significantly motivate and engage your bakery's employees. Take the time to provide constructive feedback on their work. Acknowledge their successes and celebrate milestones.

Managing a team of bakery employees can be both rewarding and challenging. By cultivating a positive work environment, training your employees, greeting customers with a smile, establishing clear goals and expectations, and providing feedback and recognition, you can empower your bakery staff to rise to the occasion and create irresistible baked goods that keep customers returning.

Retaining your employees

Retaining your employees is as vital as hiring them initially. As a business owner, you aim to keep your bakery filled with fresh cakes, treats and baked goods. To achieve this, it's crucial to ensure your team remains content and motivated.

Keep up with Technology:

Invest in a modern bakery POS system to streamline operations and enhance the customer experience.

A bakery POS system can help manage inventory, track sales, and provide efficient payment processing services.

By incorporating these strategies, you can maintain a motivated team of bakers, ensuring the continued success of your bakery business.

Expanding product lines or services

Expanding your product line

Expanding your product line marks a significant milestone in the growth of your bakery business. This strategy involves catering to your customers by introducing complementary items or variations of the products they already enjoy. Since your target audience has a vested interest in your business, seeking genuine feedback from them is crucial in the decision-making process when deciding which products and services to add.

For instance, if a mother who purchases birthday cakes suggests offering birthday candles, party hats and balloons, this valuable input aligns perfectly with your business. Similarly, if a customer inquiring about your bachelor party cakes expresses interest in sparklers, it presents a straightforward expansion that addresses specific customer needs. Grounded in market research, understanding how to diversify your product range hinges on insights from the demographic you are currently serving.

If you're considering expanding your product line, a simple initial step is to introduce easy add-ons as you conduct research on product and services that would lead to your bakery's extensions.

Guidelines for Diversifying Your Product Line

Understanding the Importance:

Expanding your product line is crucial for reaching untapped markets and attracting new customers and keeping existing customers excited and engaged. It serves as a means to enhance profitability and foster business growth. To achieve success in this endeavor, consider the following tips:

Conduct Thorough Research:

Before venturing into product line expansion, conduct comprehensive research to understand your target market. Identify their needs, preferences, and spending habits. Understand the specific products they are seeking and when they seek it. Armed with this knowledge, you can develop products tailored to resonate with your audience.

Start small

Start your bakery expansion process on a small scale. Gradually introduce new products to your line to keep costs low and minimize risks. As you establish a solid customer base, you can systematically incorporate more products into your offerings.

Test Products Before Launch:

Prior to launching any new products, conduct testing to gauge customer interest and ensure product quality. Use methods such as focus groups or surveys to gather valuable feedback. Do not skip this step as it is integral to refining your offerings before presenting them to the broader market.

Strategic Promotion:

Effectively promote your new products through well-planned marketing campaigns, leveraging social media platforms, and encouraging word-of-mouth. Enhance visibility and communicate the unique value proposition of your products to your target audience.

Continuous Evaluation and Adjustment:

Following the product launch, consistently evaluate their performance. Monitor sales metrics and gather customer feedback. If adjustments are necessary to improve sales or enhance customer satisfaction, be proactive in implementing them.

Expanding your product line holds the potential to access new markets, attract a broader customer base, and bolster your financial success. Ensure success by conducting thorough research, commencing cautiously, testing products before launch, strategic promotion, and continuous evaluation and adjustment.

Now that you have an understanding of scaling, how and when to scale, how to hire, manage staff and diversifying your product line, you have the tools needed to scale your home bakery business taking it from a dream to your reality.

CHAPTER 7: MONEY MOVES AND FINANCIAL PLANNING

Practical advice on budgeting and financial planning to ensure the sustainability of your business

When it comes to your business and money goals:

- How many cake orders do you need to receive to make that amount of money?
- How many large (multi tiered cakes), smaller (single tiered) cupcakes and or treats will allow you to make your BIG money number?
- What skills do you need to learn, add or perfect in order to make your BIG money goals?

Answer all the above questions and write them out then place it somewhere that it can be reviewed every single day. (recommended by Brendon Burchard)

Pricing for profitability

Determining the pricing for your baked goods involves more than merely matching your competitors' rates. Think about it, what does their pricing method entail? Have they also matched the pricing of someone else? How does your business differ from theirs? Your pricing should encompass not only the costs of ingredients, labor, and additional overhead such as business fees, labor and delivery but also allow for a profit. However, figuring out the precise numbers for each element can be a complex and time consuming task. How can you navigate this calculation process effectively?

Building out your pricing program will require some time. Take your time, this is the most taxing part of the pricing system. Remember once this information is imputed into your system, calculating your pricing becomes easier not to mention accurate. One of the major advantages of having a system is that you will be able to determine a base price for your products. This is the cost of your cakes before customization and added elements. This base price helps you and your customers understand the minimum or starting price to do business with you and your bakery. This amount can be added to your website and posted to your social media.

In order to properly price your cakes and baked goods there are some elements that you should ensure are covered. Let's take a close look at some of these element;

Ingredients - this is the cost of everything edible that goes into making your cakes and baked goods. Cakes, fillings, buttercreams, fondant, decorations. Every single thing.

Supplies - these are the non edible elements needed to complete your orders. We break these into the following segments:

- Cake supplies - these supplies are involved in the creation of the cake but the quantity is not easily calculated. Example, parchment paper, piping bags, plastic wrap, cooking spray, skewers. For this segment we add a percentage of the total to our cake price.
- Cake decorating supplies - these are everything that is used to create your cake. Example cake boards, dowels, cake drums (100 percent of these cost will be added to your cake order)
- Cake packaging supplies - that's everything that's needed to package the cake. Cake boxes, labels (100 percent of these cost will be added to your cake order)
- Cleaning supplies - cleaning supplies are also multiple use items in your bakery that (a percentage of your cleaning supplies will be added to each order)

Equipment - these are all the multiple use machinery and equipment needed to create our baked goods. (we add a percentage of this amount to each order)

Overhead - these are monthly fixed costs that allow your business to run but is not directly involved in creating your cakes or baked goods. Example, rent, electricity, water, CRM, canva, website hosting, accounting, banking fees, other subscription tools (the amount will be totaled and divided by the number of cakes you make per month then added to each cake in order to account for the cost)

Time/Wage - one of the most overlooked aspects of pricing for home bakers is charging for labor. Set a timer while doing each task involved in completing an order and log the time in a spreadsheet or notebook. Total the time it takes you to complete the order then multiply it by your hourly wage. This will vary based on wages in your area or on just how much you want to pay yourself or finally your level of skill. Examples of tasks, mixing, decorating, shopping, sketching, client communication, etc.

Delivery cost - delivery is priced round trip. This means the total number of miles it takes to go to and from your delivery destination. You also need to know the price per gallon of gas and how many miles your particular vehicle runs on each gallon. For example, if gas is $5 per gallon and runs 30 miles per gallon. $5 divided 30 miles is $0.17 cents per mile. If the round trip is 60 miles then multiply 60 by $0.17 giving you a round trip cost of $10.20 cents. You also need to account for the time it takes you to deliver and set up, the number of people required, toll and parking if it applies. (100 percent of the delivery fee is applied to your order)

Markup or profit - this is typically a percentage of the total cost of your cake and it's another overlooked aspect of pricing for most home bakers. Adding a markup to your cakes and baked goods allows you to save and grow your business. It covers everything from the cost of relocating to a storefront to achieving financial freedom. Making this one of the most important aspects of pricing your cakes and baked goods

Processing fees and taxes - Every CRM client management software charges a per transaction fee for processing the payments made to your business. If this cost is not included in the cost of the order then it will be deducted from your profit. Taxes vary from state to state but if this amount is not accounted for and saved then you will be responsible for the payments during tax season

Now that you have laid all the groundwork and you have a business entity, insurance and you are licensed. You have chosen a niche and you have gone over your numbers and priced you baked goods correctly;

How to build a profitable pricing strategy

Determining the pricing strategy is a pivotal aspect of your bakery business success. Striking the right balance is crucial; reasonable prices retain customers, while excessively low ones risk profitability. Creating a profitable pricing strategy is especially challenging for small home based bakery business owners.

Establishing optimal prices for products or services can be daunting for many home bakers. It necessitates retaining customers and ensuring profitability, navigating the delicate balance of setting prices that neither undercut value nor deter potential clients.

The challenge lies in finding the balance between affordability and profitability. Through diligent research, thoughtful analysis, and effective execution, business owners can confidently set prices without apprehension. A well-crafted pricing strategy empowers businesses to maintain competitiveness, achieve profitability, and foster sustainable growth over time.

Let's explore the steps to develop a profitable pricing strategy for your home bakery business:

Understand your cost:

To establish your prices effectively, it's imperative that you have a comprehensive understanding of your costs. This includes both fixed costs such as rent, utilities, salaries, and insurance, as well as variable costs associated with the materials or services necessary for your cake treats and baked goods. Knowing your expenses enables you to determine the minimum price required to cover costs and break even.

Understand your target market

Your target market plays a pivotal role in determining your pricing strategy. If your audience consists mainly of price-sensitive customers, you might need to set lower prices for your products or services. Conversely, if your target market or ideal client values quality, you should consider implementing premium pricing strategies. Additionally, employing price segmentation allows you to create tailored pricing approaches for different customer segments, enhancing your flexibility in the market.

Evaluate your competition

Assessing your competitors' pricing strategies provides valuable insights into the price points your customers might find acceptable. However, you also need to examine the rationale behind your competitors' chosen prices, consider the factors that influence their decisions. While adjusting your prices based on competitive analysis is important, exercise caution not to undervalue your offerings simply to match competitors.

Conduct price testing

Once you've identified a potential price point, conduct comprehensive testing before finalizing your pricing. Do this by engaging in market research and seeking customer feedback on your proposed prices. This helps you to determine whether your prices are perceived as too high, too low, or just right. Testing allows you to gather valuable insights, empowering you to make informed decisions and refine your pricing strategies accordingly.

Monitor and adapt

As home bakers we need to recognize that pricing is an ongoing process, requiring continuous monitoring and adaptation. Regularly analyze your pricing strategies and make adjustments as needed. Stay vigilant about changes in market conditions, shifts in customer behavior, and alterations in the competitive landscape, not to mention the ever increasing cost of ingredients and supplies. Any shifts in these factors may necessitate corresponding adjustments to your pricing strategies.

A profitable pricing strategy is indispensable for your home bakery business success. Essential elements include understanding costs, understanding your target market, analyzing competition, conducting price testing, and maintaining a proactive approach to monitoring and adjusting strategies. Regular adaptation is key, ensuring that your pricing aligns with customer expectations and sustains the profitability of your business.

Strategies for ensuring profitability

Developing effective financial management strategies for your business is vital for enhancing profitability. It involves leveraging your understanding of the key drivers that contribute to your bakery business's profits. Familiarizing yourself with financial tactics tailored to your home bakery business, aiming to boost revenue while minimizing costs.

Understanding profit drivers in your home bakery business

Profit drivers cover both the internal and external elements that influence the financial performance of your home bakery business. Understanding the dynamics of these drivers is essential for creating successful strategies to increase profitability. Concentrating on identifying and emphasizing these drivers in your home bakery business can optimize profits and yield improved growth outcomes.

- Strategies for increased revenue (as you will note this is a reiteration of so much that has been covered in this book)
- Attract New Customers: Expanding your customer base fosters business growth.
- Introduce New Product Lines: Seek input from customers on their preferences for new products or services, test their viability then add those that prove profitable.
- Target Profitable Customers: Focus on high-spending customers rather than solely increasing sales volume. Remember the 80/20 rule, 20 percent of your customers bring in 80% of your home bakeries revenue. Focus on the 20%.
- Collaborate with Top Customers: Identify key customers, understand their preferences, and tailor marketing efforts accordingly.
- Up-sell and Cross-sell: Convince customers of the advantages of more profitable products and suggest additional items.
- Explore New Markets: Utilize market research to identify opportunities for expansion into untapped areas.
- Elevate Customer Service: Enhance customer service and implement a comprehensive plan for your customer journey based on an elevated level of service.
- Adjust Prices: Regularly review product prices and consider gradual increases.
- Offer Price Discounts: Employ promotions that tie in to holidays and seasons expand the customer base.
- Boost Staff Productivity: Recognize and reward staff performance, conduct regular training sessions, and foster skill development.

Strategies for Cost Reduction:

- Manage Inventory: Implement a way to control stock in order to streamline operations and improve profit and cash flow.
- Minimize Direct Costs: Cultivate relationships with suitable suppliers, negotiate bulk purchase discounts, and avoid unnecessary expenditures.

- Reduce Indirect Costs: Minimize waste, increase staff efficiency, and employ low-cost marketing techniques.
- Trim Overheads: Identify cost-saving opportunities in areas such as energy consumption and supplier selection.
- Eliminate Unprofitable Products/Services: Concentrate on popular offerings with the highest gross profit margins, remove menu items that are not profitable or cause a time drain.
- Benchmark Financials: Compare business costs, such as rent and utilities, with industry peers to identify areas for improvement.

Money Mindset

Let's take a deeper look at your money mindset and how it affects your life and business.

Money mindset in particular is your beliefs about money. It includes how you think about money and greatly influences how much you charge for your cakes, how you save, spend, manage your debt and of vital importance your belief about your earning potential as a home based baker.

For example, believing that $150 is the most someone will pay you for a cake or believing that by taking a few classes and courses you can improve your skill enough to systematically increase your price point as your skill improves will actually affect your skill, how you work and how much you're willing to grow your business.

It's important to understand the origin of how we think about money. How did we develop a mindset of lack or abundance? This quite often ties into our childhood, the views of our caretakers and continues into adulthood based on the views of those in our circle. Do they view money as private, shameful and not to be talked about or do they openly discuss money.

Your money mindset includes:

- What you personally think that you can or cannot do with money ("money cannot buy happiness", I think we have all heard that one)
- How much money you think you deserve or that you deserve to charge for your cakes or baked goods.
- Your beliefs about how you should manage your money. (are you aware of your monthly expenses?, what's due/ when? or does money

just go unchecked into or out of your account) how you spend, save or donate.

- How you believe you should pay-off or manage your debt.
- Your beliefs about your ability to grow your wealth. ("God will provide", that's a very popular one)
- Your confidence in your ability to be financially stable.

Do you have a scarcity mindset or an abundance mindset?

As a self-taught baker it's important to determine if your mindset is negative meaning based on scarcity or positive meaning based on abundance.

Let's discuss some signs of a scarcity mindset:

- Living cake order to cake order
- The thought of your finances makes overwhelmed and doubtful of your abilities
- You are filled with guilt from financial mistakes you made in the past
- You're feeling stuck from fear of failure
- You are envious of other because of their perceived successes
- Believing there isn't enough money to invest in your skill

If any of the signs above resonate with you then it's time to shift your mindset from negative to positive. Let's discuss a few ways that this can be done.

1.   Examine your financial perspective

Before you can successfully move forward and make changes in your life and finances it is important to reflect on past financial decisions and see how it has influenced your present choices. Really consider your experiences with money up to this point.

- How were you raised to perceive money?
- Were you taught to treat money as a possession or an experience?
- How important was money growing up? Did its lack or abundance directly impact your happiness?
- Were your parents/guardians spenders, savers or was there a healthy balance?
- Did they struggle to acquire money?

- While growing up were you widely exposed to different classes of money?

A major key to making better choices in the future is to deeply consider and examine everything that has influenced how you view money today. This is not an excuse to assign blame to yourself or those that helped shape who you have become AKA your parents or guardians. Instead this is an exercise to better understand the foundation of why you made the choice and reframe your approach to money going forward.

2.   Acquire a positive money mindset

One of the ways that this can be done is by changing your perspective on finances and adopting a positive money mindset through financial affirmations. Create a positive mindset by Journaling, meditating, and visualizing your future. In order to see results you also need to do the work by making sure your skill set is up to par and making sure you are constantly working to improve your craft. Words have power and the way you talk to yourself about money plays a very big role in how you approach your finances. It is important to pay attention to what you say to yourself when money comes to you (eg. when you get paid for a cake order)

A few key times to take note of your thoughts are:

- When money is used to cover your necessities such as bills, food, healthcare, etc.
- When you spend on yourself
- When you make financial mistakes
- When speaking about your finances with others

If any of these circumstances ends with you talking negatively to yourself then it's time to reframe the script. Think of ways that you can speak to yourself in a more positive way. Some money mantra ideas are:

I"ll always live cake order to cake order." reframe that to _____ I can update my pricing to reflect the value of my cakes so that i can comfortably cover my expenses and not feel so drained at the end of the month."

I'll never make as much money as my colleagues." reframe that to _____ we are all at different stages in our career and that's ok. I will learn, grow, improve my skill and business techniques while periodically increasing the prices of my cakes.

I fail to use my money wisely. Reframe that to _____ I have made mistakes with my money. Everyone makes mistakes. I will use it as a learning opportunity and make better decisions going forward.

3.   Shift your mindset from spender to saver

It is important to determine your financial values and goals. These will help you guide your choices and shift your mindset from one of spending to one of saving. These values and goals will reinforce what is important to you and how you see yourself and your finances in the future for example 5 or 10 years from now.

Questions to ask yourself to help you set financial goals and values.

- Do I have an emergency fund in place?
- What financial risks threaten my money goals?
- How do I want to make an impact with people or causes in my community? Financially?
- Do I have major purchases planned in the next 3-5 years?
- What quality of life do I desire?
- What are my goals for myself and my cake business?
- How and when do I envision retirement?
- Do I want to leave a financial legacy to my family?

Now that you have determined your financial goals and values how will you make them happen? What tasks need to be accomplished to reach those goals? Really think about what needs to be done, break them down into steps and break each step down into minute tasks then work to accomplish one task at a time.

4.   Become aware of and monitor your spending.

One of the best ways to learn more about how you use your money and to be able to adjust your money mindset is by tracking your spending over the course of the coming months. Monitor the money that goes in and out of your account. How much and when? A key step is to monitor your emotions while tracking, spending and saving your money.

Do this by asking yourself the following questions.

- How do you feel when you get paid for an order?
- Or when you pay your bills or purchase cake decorating necessities?
- How do you feel when you spend money on yourself? Your family? Others?
- What are your spending triggers?
- How do you feel about yourself when you spend as a result of being triggered?

Keeping a journal during the period you are monitoring your spending will help.

5. Make a commitment to yourself to change your money habits.

Once you have made that commitment to change your money mindset there is no other way but to actually do the work and follow through. Remember this will not be an easy task so write and rewrite your values and goals often. Keep them close and constantly refer back to them especially during tough times. Believe in yourself and your abilities. Show gratitude daily for life and how far you have come. You got this!

How I overcame the 'You shouldn't charge that much you work from home" and started charging what I was worth.

Now my initial thought was I never asked you to buy from me. But the truth of the matter is that I did. By simply being a business that exists in the world I'm asking people to hand over their hard earned cash in exchange for cakes and treats that I produce. I need to convey my value to my customers and potential customers because while my price point means that not everyone can purchase my products their value should not be a question.

" I would like to place an order for my birthday cake myself because my friends won't order a cake from you from my birthday, they said you're too expensive"
" they're getting me a cake from Miss Maxwell or a $200 sheet cake from cake man raven"

This statement from a client that ordered ALL of her friends' custom birthday cakes from my bakery and paid for it herself. Now she was ordering her own cake and asking me to say it was a gift because all she wanted was an A's Exquisite Cakes birthday cake.

Am I conveying the value of my cakes, treats and baked goods? What is the value of my products? How is my business positioned in the market? What problems do I solve for my clients? Can I be relied on to deliver on promises my business makes?

Once I was able to answer these questions the "expensive" label impacted me differently. If by saying I'm expensive you mean that my bakery business consistently provides great tasting cakes, treats and baked goods. Or that we created lasting memories for our clients both in taste and visuals. Maybe that our designs are clean, modern, elegant, detailed and we deliver on time. We address the concerts of our clients, listen to our clients problems and offer solutions. Then yes, the label of expensive fits my bakery. I offer a product of superior value and deliver on said promises.

A mentor once told me if you're not scared to send the invoice then it's not the right price.

Once I was able to clearly understand my own value I was then able to communicate it to my clients and that enabled me to move away from the constant need to defend my business and just say "My price is my price

CHAPTER 8: ACHIEVING A 6-FIGURE INCOME

Detailed strategies on how to take your baking business to a 6-figure income, including upselling, cross-selling, and premium pricing

Strategies for increasing revenue in your bakery business

Increasing sales and revenue stands as a top priority for every bakery business. Of utmost importance is focusing on your bakery's customers and their response to your diverse sales and marketing strategies. This aids in determining the most effective methods for driving increased sales and revenue. Strategic marketing and advertising campaigns play a pivotal role in both attracting new customers and retaining existing ones, thereby contributing to the bakeries overall profit.

1. Set measurable goals - Establish measurable objectives for the extent to which your bakery aims to increase its sales and revenue. This makes it possible for you to create a clear strategy for pursuing your goals and selecting the methods that align with your objectives.

2. Focus on repeat customers (Prioritize repeat customers) - Nurture connections with customers who have shone loyalty to your bakery brand through multiple or repeat purchases. Increased communication serves to reinforce your bakery in their minds and enables you to shape the message they receive. Explore other methods of communication such as email or text messages to highlight sales or introduce new inventory. Utilize email systems that provide metrics, such as open rates and link clicks, allowing you to track the effectiveness of your communication and marketing strategies.

3. Add new bakery products or services - To boost sales from existing customers, consider expanding your product range to include new menu items that cater to their needs. Explore seasonal products that align with your holidays or seasons such as pumpkin cakes during fall season.

4   Monitor and adjust your pricing plan - To increase revenue in your bakery business without altering the volume of sales, reassess your pricing strategy. Lowering prices might attract more buyers and secure a larger market share from competitors, while raising prices could be viable if your brand carries substantial value and customer belief.

5   Bundle your bakery products or services - Promoting bundled products can incentivize customers to make additional purchases as they can save money by buying multiple items together. Bundling bakery items involves packaging items together and presenting them as a cohesive set for example bundling cakes plus treats. Alternatively, you can provide a discount when customers choose to purchase multiple items together.

6.   Add alternative methods of payment - Boosting sales might be achievable by introducing new payment methods that cater to customer convenience. Are there popular methods of payment options within the bakery industry that you're not currently incorporating, and consider setting up the necessary infrastructure to accommodate any methods not currently accepted, such as credit cards, cash exchange apps, or apple pay.

7.   Add a delivery charge - Certain customers may be inclined to pay a higher price for their cakes, treats or baked goods if it includes delivery. For local deliveries, consider employing a set delivery fee per area.

8.   Increase the area you serve - Consider expanding the geographic range of your customers by increasing the distance to which you deliver or provide services. Additionally, consider advertising in neighboring communities.

9.   Reach out to past clients - Reacquiring previous customers often requires less effort than acquiring new ones. Add a segment to your marketing strategy tailored to former customers, this allows you to approach them differently than your current customer base. Entice them with specific incentives, such as discounts on new purchases. Former customers can also provide valuable referrals or reviews, contributing to the attraction of new customers, former clients can also

provide your bakery business with reviews showcasing their customer experience with your bakery.

10. Offer subscriptions - Your baker could generate more sales by offering a monthly subscription service for example cake of the month club where you offer a different flavor monthly. This can automate sales for your bakery and bring in recurring revenue.

11. Niche Markets: Identify and cater to niche markets. This could be gluten-free products, vegan baking, or specialty cakes.

12. Catering and Bulk Orders: Tap into the catering market for events, businesses, and schools.

13. Retail Partnerships: Partner with local cafes, restaurants, and stores to sell your products.

14. Online Sales: Develop an online store to reach a broader market, including national or international customers.

Upselling, cross-selling, and premium pricing

Ways to increase sales in your home bakery

Upselling

Upselling in your bakery business is offering your customers a more valuable and higher-priced version of the baked goods they are looking for. For example by showing customers that other better designed or more detailed versions that may better fulfill their needs, bakeries can increase average order values while helping customers leave more satisfied with their order. When it comes to sales techniques to grow your bakeries average sales, a product upsell may be one of the best approaches. Upselling has many benefits to retailers, from building deeper relationships with customers by suggesting premiums or upgrades that will eventually deliver more value, to making customers feel like they got the better deal, encouraging them to come back for more.

Example of upselling: A customer contacts your bakery to purchase a ballerina themed cake for her daughter's birthday. After pricing the basic inspiration design she offered you suggest the addition of ballerina slippers, tutu and sheet music to the cake. This makes for a more detailed design that incorporates more of the theme while increasing the price of the cake order. Even though the cake is now more expensive, the customer is more satisfied with the purchase.

Cross selling

Cross-selling in your bakery business is recommending several products related to the original purchase of the customers. After the customer has decided to purchase a cake, treats or baked goods, it's up to you to show them how other products might add value, save them time, or save trips to other stores. The add-on items that you choose to cross-sell can be complementary products to help the customer enjoy their first product even more. For example if the customer orders a cake you can suggest the purchase of cupcakes, cake pops and other treats to build out their treat table.

Example of cross selling: While having a discussion with the client who purchased the ballerina cake it comes to light that she also intends to incorporate a treat table into the party decor so you suggest the addition of cake pops, rice crispy treats, chocolate covered oreos and push pops all decorated in the ballerina theme. You have now become a one stop shop for all of her cake and treat table needs while again increasing the customer spend with your bakery business.

Premium pricing

What is a premium brand?

Defining a 'premium' brand can be challenging as it changes based on the perspective of the individual being asked. Each person has their own unique set of values and priorities, resulting in differing opinions on what makes a brand premium.

A premium brand is typically perceived as an individual, company, product, or service that holds an elevated status, distinctive quality, or exceptional value in the eyes of its target audience or ideal client.

These brands offer a blend of excellent quality, value, purpose, and an outstanding overall customer experience. While many associate a premium brand with a higher price, it's important to note that price alone does not define what makes a brand truly 'premium" or luxury.

Generally, premium brands have distinct characteristics and qualities that convey a sense of elevation.

- Quality

As a premium brand you cannot simply state your superiority; you must substantiate it in some manner. Consumers typically evaluate the quality of cakes, treats and baked goods based on factors like taste, quality, exceptional decor, and reliability. Traits such as high-quality ingredients, and innovative design serve as benchmarks informing purchasing decisions. When perceived as the best in their field, cake decorators are more likely to command higher prices.

- Price

Ironically, most consumers often rely on price as an indicator of quality. In the consumer mindset, there exists a perceived correlation between the price of your cakes, treats and baked goods or service and its inherent quality. Alternatively, if the price fails to align with their expectations of quality, they may class your product or service as either "too expensive" or "not worth the cost." The underlying psychology here suggests that if an offer appears too good to be true, skepticism is warranted.

- Value

Customers seek optimal value for their money.

In order to command higher prices for your cakes, treats and baked goods, customers must perceive that the value they receive far surpasses the amount they pay. However, similar to quality, the concept of value is often subjective and open to interpretation.

Many cake businesses just think they understand why customers value their products and services. In contrast, a premium brand dedicates time, effort and resources to comprehensively understanding their customers' desires and expectations. With this insight, they can craft offerings that deliver multiple layers of benefits, extending beyond what is expected.

How to grow your cake business successfully

- Develop a growth plan

In the competitive landscape of the home bakery business, achieving increased profits often goes hand in hand with business growth. An expansion strategy serves as the business's roadmap for achieving this growth, whether it involves widening the customer base, diversifying menu offerings, enhancing profit margins, bolstering brand presence, or moving into a brick-and-mortar commerce location.

A bakery business growth strategy plan is a plan to increase the bakeries size and value.

- Define your targeted growth areas

While aspiring to expand your bakery business is commendable, it's vital to specify the areas you intend to develop. Your bakery's growth plan should precisely focus on the particular areas that you would like to expand. Some of the potential focal points for strategic growth include:

- ✓ Hiring employees
- ✓ Moving to a brick and mortar storefront space
- ✓ Establishing new locations for your bakery business
- ✓ Introducing new products and/or services
- ✓ Broadening purchase locations for example launching an online store
- ✓ Expanding the customer base and or improving the rate at which you acquire new customers

It's pausable for your growth plan to include more than one of the initiatives mentioned above, as effective growth often involves an interconnected approach. For instance, boosting product sales can lead to increased revenue, making it necessary for the addition of new locations and personnel to support the surge in sales.

- Conduct Market and Industry Research

Once you've identified the specific areas for growth in your bakery, it's imperative to prove that this is the best choice and assess the feasibility of such growth.

Conducting thorough research into the current state of your industry provides invaluable insights to determine the necessity and viability of the area of your desired growth. This can involve activities such as conducting surveys and focus groups with both existing and potential customers.

The information and insights gained during this phase will serve as the foundation for establishing expectations and growth objectives for your home bakery. This, in turn, allows you to determine a realistic timeline, budget, and ultimate goal.

- Establish Growth Goals

After identifying the areas and reasons for growth, the next crucial step is quantifying how much growth is possible.

These goals should always align with your ultimate desire for where you envision your home bakery, yet they must also be practical and capable of being attained. The insights gained from industry research play a pivotal role in setting goals that have a base in reality.

Finally, take the initiative to quantify your goals in terms of metrics and timelines. For instance, aiming to "increase sales by 30% quarter-over-quarter for the next three years" provides much clearer direction than a more generalized goal of "increasing sales."

Develop a strategic plan for your course of action

Subsequently, outline the steps you will take to reach your home bakeries growth objectives through a comprehensive growth strategy. This plan should cover a set of tasks, associated deadlines, assigned teams or responsible individuals, and the required resources for accomplishing your growth goals.

Identify the tools and necessary prerequisites for growing your home bakery

Before implementing your plan, the final phase involves identifying the essential requirements you will need throughout the process. These specific resources are vital for achieving your growth goals more efficiently and accurately. Examples include:

1. Funding: Organizations like banks might require a capital investment or an internal budget allocation to successfully execute this project.

2. Tools & Software: determine the technological resources necessary to streamline and gain insights during the growth process.

3. Services: Enhance your growth potential by considering the assistance of consultants that specialize in the field of home bakeries.

Implement your plan

Having completed all the necessary planning, resource allocation, and goal-setting, you are now prepared to execute your bakery's growth plan and generate results for the business.

Throughout this implementation phase, it's crucial to hold yourself accountable, maintain open lines of communication with your consultant, and regularly assess initial results against your forecasted growth goals. This allows you to determine if your projected results are still attainable or if any adjustments are needed.

CHAPTER 9: BUDGETING AND FINANCIAL PLANNING

Practical advice on budgeting and financial planning to ensure the sustainability of your business

Understanding budgeting in your bakery business

Business budgeting is the process of creating and overseeing a financial document that forecasts income and expenses for a specific period, for example quarterly or yearly. This critical skill is essential for bakery business owners to ensure that their bakery has the necessary resources to execute initiatives and achieve their goals.

What makes up a basic budget?

A basic budget comprises projected income and expenses for a given timeframe, such as a quarter or a year. After deducting expenses from projected income, the remaining funds can be allocated to various projects and initiatives, this aids in preventing overspending. Comparing past budgets to actual financial performance provides valuable insights for future planning.

Types of Budgeting:

Several budgeting types prioritize different factors in financial planning. These include:

- Zero-Based Budgeting: Sets each item at zero dollars initially before reallocating.
- Static Budgeting or Incremental-Based Budgeting: Uses data from your bakeries past years to adjust the upcoming period's budget.
- Performance-Based Budgeting: Uses cash flow per unit of product or service.
- Activity-Based Budgeting: Begins with the company's goals and works backward to determine the cost of achieving them.
- Value Proposition Budgeting: Assumes no line item is included unless it directly adds value to the bakery.

The correct budgeting type for your business depends on the bakery's circumstances, and experimentation may be necessary to find the ideal fit.

The importance of budgeting in your home bakery business

1.   Ensures Resource Availability: Primarily, budgeting ensures that an organization has sufficient resources to meet its goals. Planning finances in advance allows for the allocation of resources to marketing and other initiatives while identifying areas for potential cost-cutting.

2.   Facilitates Goal Setting and Reporting: Budgeting goes beyond allocating the money that will be spent; it aids in setting, reporting and tracking of internal goals. Financial goals, aligned with the chosen budgeting method, guide the allocation of expenses and inform monetary needs.

3.   Helps with Project Prioritization: Budgeting requires prioritizing projects and initiatives. Whether using value proposition budgeting or another method, it forces you to consider return on investment (ROI), alignment with company values, and impact on broader financial goals.

4.   Open Financing Opportunities: Showing a history of documented budgetary information is crucial for startups or those seeking external investors. Investors value clear financial performance data, including budgeted and actual spend from previous periods.

5.   Provides a Pivotal Plan: if we have learnt nothing from the recent pandemic, we have learnt the need to pivot and add additional streams of income to our bakery business. A budget serves as a financial roadmap, but the bakery business landscape is unpredictable. A well-thought-out budget allows for agility in the face of unforeseen circumstances, enabling home bakeries to pivot and navigate challenges effectively.

In summary, business budgeting is a dynamic and strategic process that plays a pivotal role in financial planning, goal setting, and the overall success of your home bakery business.

Guide to Developing a Business Budget

Creating a business budget involves several essential steps to ensure financial stability and facilitate informed decision-making in your home bakery business. Here's a step-by-step guide:

1.   Calculate Revenue:

- Include all revenue streams over the past 12 months this determines your bakeries monthly income.
- For new businesses, research industry standards to estimate revenue.

2.   Sum Up Fixed Costs (Overhead):

- Identify fixed costs, such as rent, payroll, and debt repayment, canva, accounting.
- Compile these costs to understand the consistent financial commitments.

3.   Determine Variable Costs:

- Identify variable costs, including utilities, billable labor, materials, transaction fees, and commissions.
- Variable costs can fluctuate based on the bakeries business activity.

4.   Subtract Fixed and Variable Costs:

- Subtract total fixed and variable costs from revenue to determine the cost of producing goods or services.
- This calculation impacts net income—the amount left after deducting all expenses and taxes.

5.   Set Aside a Just-in-Case Fund:

- Allocate funds for unexpected costs, such as equipment replacements.
- This reserve acts as a financial buffer for unforeseen circumstances.

6.   Create a Profit and Loss Statement:

- Sum up all income and expenses for the month.
- Subtract total expenses from income to determine profit or loss.

- A positive result signifies profit, while a negative result indicates a loss.

7.   Utilize Budgeting Tools:

- Explore online budgeting templates or use accounting software like QuickBooks® for a more structured approach.
- Templates and software streamline the budgeting process, providing a foundation for financial planning.

8.   Making Informed Decisions Using Your Budget:

- Make the budget a regular resource in your decision-making process.
- Regularly consult the budget when making spending decisions.
- Use the budget as a reality check to ensure adherence to financial limits.
- Discipline in budget management positions the business for sustainable growth.

By following these steps and integrating the budget into your daily financial decision-making routine, you can establish financial discipline and position your bakery business for both current success and future growth.

Financial planning strategies

A Comprehensive Business and Personal Financial Planning Guide

Balancing personal and business goals is an important step in the financial planning process of your home bakery. It involves setting both short and long-term goals, ensuring harmony between business expansion objectives and your personal financial aspirations. Finding and striking a balance is imperative for sustained financial success, preventing potential conflicts that could hinder the long-term goals of your home bakery business.

- Explore Financing Alternatives:

When starting, expanding or dealing with the day to day realities of running a home bakery business. Money is always at the forefront of all decision making.

In order to secure the necessary capital to start, expand or run your home bakery, consider personal savings, external funding example loans, or customer contributions. Leveraging customer support for financing, such as advance payments or product/service exchanges, can be a cost-effective strategy.

- Control Costs:

In order to ensure profitability of your home bakery it's necessary to generate revenue exceeding expenses. Prioritizing cost control helps to identify operational efficiencies, and enhance productivity. Successful bakeries often focus on cost management to drive financial sustainability especially during times of financial hardship.

- Manage Liquidity:

Maintaining healthy cash flow is necessary for sustained growth in your home bakery. Establish disciplined systems for managing receivables and payables. Create a cash buffer for emergencies to enhance liquidity management for example start a business emergency fund.

- Manage Taxes:

Filing and paying taxes is a necessary part of running a home bakery business. In order to navigate the complexities of tax laws, seek professional advice from accountants, lawyers or tax professionals to ensure that your business is always compliant. Choose a legal status that aligns with your business goals to optimize tax benefits. Keep meticulous records, meet filing deadlines, and consider professional bookkeeping software for accurate tax management.

- Manage Risk:

When operating a bakery business it is necessary to address diverse sources of risk, including business, operational, financial, and disability risks. Stay vigilant about external threats such as new competitors, technological changes, and regulatory requirements. Implement a solid financial strategy, build buffers, and manage cash to withstand unforeseen financial threats.

- Establish a Retirement Plan:

One of the biggest reasons for the pivot of my business is to ensure retirement and secure long-term financial stability. Explore alternatives like, SEP IRAs, or SIMPLE IRAs, with a focus on maximizing contribution allowances.

- Build a Safety Net:

Diversify assets to minimize concentrated risk tied to personal businesses. Asset diversification across various sectors, regions, and assets decreases overall portfolio risk.

- Start Estate Planning:

Consider creating an estate plan to arrange asset disposal after passing. Develop family trusts, personal wills, and address financial, tax, and medical considerations. Optimize estate planning to reduce uncertainties, lower taxes, and maximize the estate's value (Home bakery business).

- Plan for Business Succession:

Consider creating a robust bakery business succession plan addressing interests of co- owners (if any), employees, clients, and other stakeholders. Consider tax and financial implications associated with your bakery business succession. Tailor the plan's complexity to the business's size, industry, and legal status. Enlist the help of a legal representative to ensure that the process is smooth and correctly executed.

Adopting these comprehensive financial planning steps when planning for your home bakeries financial future, ensures a holistic approach, aligning personal and business financial objectives for sustained success and long-term prosperity.

CHAPTER 10: ESSENTIAL BAKING SKILLS

As the sole employee of your business you need to be knowledgeable of both the front of house and backhouse of your business. Meaning that you need to be able to answer questions about why using fresh ingredients like eggs, butter and milk produces a better bakery product while as a back of house employee you need to be able to correctly measure your ingredients and follow recipe directions. Remember baking is a science. You need to know your products. How the ingredients work together, which ingredients work best for you, how your batter tastes, how it smells while baking and the taste and moisture content that should be expected after baking. When you know your products inside out you can effectively explain it to others.

Baking Skills Mastery

Successfully achieving a baking career path demands a specific skill set. Knowledge of some of these crucial skills and baking terminology can be acquired through education and or apprenticeships. These skills enable proficiency in all areas of baking and decorating   the production of high-quality baked goods and making it possible for profitability. Soft skills refer to character traits that facilitate effective interaction with others and the efficient execution of tasks. These skills play a vital role in delivering excellent customer service to clients and fostering positive working relationships with team members.

9 Skills you need to succeed as a cake decorator

- Baking and Cake Decorating Skills: It's crucial to have strong baking and cake decorating skills. You need to have a solid understanding of baking techniques, such as measuring ingredients accurately, mixing and blending, and baking times and temperatures. To have a good eye for design and be able to create beautiful visually appealing cakes and desserts.

- Time Management Skills: Time management is critical for success. You need to be able to manage your time effectively to ensure that you can produce high-quality products while also handling other aspects of your business, such as marketing, administration, and customer service.

- Business and Marketing Skills: As a self-taught baker, you are not only responsible for baking and decorating cakes but also for running a business. You need to have a good understanding of business and marketing principles, including pricing, sales, customer service, and branding. You need to be able to effectively market your products and services to attract customers and grow your business.

- Customer service: many bakers are sole proprietors and therefore tasked with directly handling customer orders. Possessing outstanding customer service skills is instrumental in fostering positive relationships and building a strong rapport with clientele. Creating an environment where individuals feel comfortable and valued constitutes a crucial aspect of effective customer service. For instance, providing exceptional customer service could involve offering clients unique, custom baked products, potentially encouraging them to continue to patronize your home bakery.

- Creative and Innovative Thinking Skills: To stand out in the competitive baking industry, you need to be creative and innovative in your baking and cake decorating. You need to be able to come up with unique and exciting ideas that will attract customers and set you apart from your competitors.

- Communication: Effective communication skills are important for bakers to establish successful connections with suppliers, vendors, customers, and team members.

Skilled communication involves articulating thoughts clearly, employing appropriate non-verbal cues, and actively listening especially while taking clients' orders. The ability to communicate effectively is crucial for the success of any bakery business.

Customer service

- Problem Solving Skills: As a self-taught baker, you will encounter various challenges and problems along the way. You need to have strong problem-solving skills to effectively handle any issues that may arise. This includes being able to troubleshoot problems with baking and decorating, resolving customer complaints, and managing business-related issues

- Precision: Cake decorating requires sharp focus and attention to detail to ensure the immaculate consistency of designs. This attention to detail aids in crafting custom designs that harmonize seamlessly with the overall showpiece and plan for the event.

- Structure: Cake decorators need to possess excellent organizational skills to maintain a tidy workspace, efficiently handle inventory, monitor supplies, and establish deadlines for both custom and standard orders ensuring the work week runs smoothly.

Techniques and tips for improving these skills

Tips to enhance your skills:

- Research: Building a thriving bakery requires a willingness to learn, grow and constantly improve. Utilize online resources and explore recipe books to grasp new techniques and processes. This gives you a competitive edge making it possible to stay ahead of the competition.
- Skill over flash. Work diligently to improve your skill instead of chasing flashy tools that promise to magically make your work better.
- Network with fellow bakers and industry professionals: Connecting with other bakers in the industry can be a source of inspiration for your career development. Sharing recipes and success tips can contribute to skill enhancement, other bakers can also offer support and advice by helping you troubleshoot issues in your bakery.
- Master the basics: Contrary to popular belief you don't need a ton of recipes to start your home bakery business. Before jumping head first into complex recipes, master the fundamental baking techniques, tweak and test them until you get consistent results in taste, texture, moisture etc. A strong foundation in basic recipes and techniques forms the cornerstone of advanced skill development. Build your buttercream technique. Get comfortable with applying buttercream to your cake. Learn to troubleshoot and fix issues with your buttercream cakes. It's a common misconception that fondant hides the imperfections in your buttercream but that isn't the case, fondant actually enhances the imperfections in your buttercream.

- Preparation is key. Read and become familiar with your recipes, pre-measure all the ingredients and have them ready before starting, have all your tools cleaned and ready. Good preparation gives you the best chance of accuracy and consistency when baking. Prep your pans before mixing your recipe so that your batter can be divided evenly once ready. At every stage of the baking process it's essential to be prepared for the next step.

- Mistakes as a learning experience: In the initial stages of entering the bakery industry, hell at every stage, you will encounter challenges or unintended outcomes from recipes. Embrace these mistakes as learning opportunities, breaking down and understanding why mistakes happen paves the way for continuous improvement.

- Create a plan or design: At the beginning of our cake design journey we spend so much time assembling and finishing our blank canvas that we often forget that the cake still needs to be decorated, then we're often at a loss as to where to place the decor elements or how to finish our cake design.

- Confidence is key: There is no quick way to gain confidence as a baker or cake decorator. Confidence comes with time and repetition, as you learn to work through baking issues, learn to make tweaks and fix problems. Once you begin getting consistent results your confidence will slowly grow.

- Master fondant skills: Despite initial apprehension, working with fondant expands your design possibilities and enhances your portfolio, offering more options to clients. So many bakers are afraid of working with fondant and often complain about the time it takes to learn and perfect, however working with fondant can add so much range and design possibilities to your portfolio and brings additional design possibilities to what you can offer to your clients.

Basic Baking Tips You Can't Ignore:

- Always follow the recipe. I know this sounds very basic but until you have tried the recipe as it was originally developed you won't know what changes can be made. A menu item should not be added until you can regularly produce it in all the various sizes that you offer with consistent quality, meaning consistent taste, texture, moisture etc. This gives your bakery an edge and helps you to stand out in the baking industry.

- Measurement is key to consistency: Weight measurements are more accurate than cups and help with the consistency of your baked goods.

- Bake with room temperature ingredients. Ingredients like eggs, milk and butter need to be at room temperature. The ingredients shouldn't be warm but still cool to the touch. The butter for instance should indent when pressed with your thumb. This can be achieved after 1-2 hours out of the refrigerator.

- Sift your dry ingredients before mixing. Sifting your dry ingredients together then thoroughly mixing together helps you to evenly incorporate your ingredients.

- Don't over mix your ingredients. Over mixing causes cakes and baked goods to be tough, this is because it removes most of the air added in during the creaming process.

- Don't under mix your batter. Under mixing prevents the ingredients from being incorporated together.

- Lining your baking pans with parchment paper allows the cake to release easily after baking. You can purchase parchment rounds in the size of your pans pre-cut or you can cut them yourself from parchment sheets/rolls.

- Preheat your oven for 20 minutes before baking. That allows your oven to be properly heated to the correct temperature before baking.

- Don't open the oven often during baking. Every time you open and close the door the oven has to get back to the set baking temperature, instead set a timer for 5-10 min before baking time in order to start checking for doneness.

- Your cake is baked when a taster, skewer or knife is inserted into the middle and comes out clean.

- If your oven is not convection then bake on the center rack.

- Do not over crowd your oven. Too many cakes in your oven leads to longer baking time

- Do not overfill your baking pans. This may lead to a few outcomes, longer baking time, denser cakes, the edges of the cakes being burnt as the middle takes longer to bake, spillover of batter onto the pans and the oven.

- For moist cakes remove front the cake pan and wrap in plastic wrap while still warm then allow to come to room temperature.
- Always cool your cakes for a few hours or overnight before decorating.
- When using soft fillings use ganache or buttercream to pipe an dam around the inside edge of your cake layers. If using buttercream and the filling is very soft, pipe two dams.
- Mix slowly. When making your buttercream, after adding the butter switch to the paddle attachment and reduce the mixer speed to low in order to remove the air bubbles.
- Internal structure of tiered cakes is key. In order to keep your cakes in the most perfect condition during delivery and display make sure that the internal structure is sound.
- Alternate the dowels. When adding dowels to your cake do not add them in one row but alternate inside and out in order to balance and support the weight of the cakes above.
- Secure the cake to the cake board. Ensure that the cake is stuck or secure to the cake board in order to prevent movement during delivery.
- Add a center dowel to your cake. Adding a center dowel to your cake helps to keep your cake together and to prevent movement during delivery.
-]When carrying your boxed cake place a hand at the bottom of the box to carry most of the weight.
- When transporting your cake, create a clear flat space in your vehicle free of rolling objects.
- Keep the transport vehicle cool. It is important to keep the cake cool during delivery; this helps with stability and to prevent delivery mishaps.
- Cake tastes best at room temperature so allow for optimal cooling time before serving. (Approximately 1-2 hours depending on the size of the cake)

Techniques and tips for improving these skills

Establishing a weekly routine is crucial for maintaining productivity and maximizing your workday efficiency. Break down your weekly tasks into smaller segments and allocate them to specific days. Be sure to factor in time for lunch, cleanup, and strategic rest breaks.

Regularly assess your progress by the end of each week (let's call it "Cake Week Monday"). Reflect on what went smoothly, identify areas for improvement, and evaluate whether tasks adhered to the schedule. Consider delegating time-consuming tasks and pinpoint any skill gaps that need attention.

Remember that confidence develops gradually. Prioritize progress over perfection, recognizing that confidence is a byproduct of addressing challenges in your cake decorating projects. Also consistent practice is key. Visualize and mentally walk through the cake decorating process regularly. Integrate practice sessions into your weekly schedule to hone your skills.

Avoid overwhelming yourself. While pushing creative boundaries is important, refrain from accepting cake projects beyond your current skill level. Taking on tasks outside your expertise can lead to stress and self-doubt. If there's sufficient time before the order deadline, use it to develop the necessary skills through focused practice.

Test your menu items thoroughly before offering them to the public. Refine recipes until you achieve consistent results. Incorporate product development or recipe testing days into your schedule for continuous improvement.

Establish systems and processes for your cake decorating tasks. Familiarize yourself with each step, practicing until it becomes second nature. Make these processes a reflexive part of your routine.

Prioritize mastering fundamental techniques over chasing trending cake designs. A strong foundation in basic skills will empower you to tackle any popular or innovative cake design that comes your way.

The role of creativity in baking

A genuine passion for baking extends to a deep understanding of flavor combinations that complement a diverse range of cakes, treats and baked goods. Channeling your curiosity about the fusion of different ingredients and exploring the resulting outcomes is crucial. Bakers leverage their skills to experiment with diverse flavors and employ various cake decorating techniques, ranging from simple shapes to intricate fondant designs and gumpaste flowers. The level of creativity of each individual baker plays a pivotal role in their ability to craft innovative tastes and flavors for baked goods, as well as in designing visually appealing cake decorations.

Bakers and cake decorators use their creativity to create stunning designs that complement their baked goods. They incorporate their understanding of color, shape and other visual aesthetic principles to make their cakes, treats and baked goods as appealing as possible.

To stand out in the competitive baking industry, you need to be creative and innovative in your baking and cake decorating. You need to be able to come up with unique and exciting ideas that will attract customers and set you apart from your competitors.

It's not enough to follow the current trends, think outside the box and be creative with your designs. This keeps your customers engaged while helping to convert new fans into paying customers

Techniques for fostering creativity

Understanding baking theory

Mastering the art of baking begins with a solid grasp of its fundamental theory, fortunately, you can acquire this knowledge through books and in person or online classes. As self-taught bakers, it's crucial to have strong baking and cake decorating skills. You need to have a solid understanding of techniques, such as measuring ingredients accurately, mixing and blending, baking times and temperatures. Once you have a solid foundation in the basic skills, you are now prepared to start your journey as a cake decorator.

- Start simple then branch out

Every journey begins with a small step, and that includes stepping into the world of baking. I understand your dream of crafting exquisite cakes, treats and baked goods similar to those created by mentors, friends and other cake decorators. However, to achieve the skill required for such creations, you must first start simply at the very beginning, experimentation and master the basics. Then add more complicated techniques and skills as you grow and become more confident.

- Learn from and be mentored by others

To continue building and enhancing your baking techniques, consider being mentored by those who have mastered their craft or are further along in the process than you are. Research mentors in your chosen field or those who have mastered certain skills that you would like to improve upon. Do they offer classes or courses, online or in person, do they have a mentorship program? utilize YouTube and other search engines in order to access baking tutorials by seasoned experts.

- Make it a business

Fortune favors the brave or those with a willingness to take the leap and act. So many bakers and cake decorators believe they need to be experts to start their bakery business, but becoming an expert takes time, and if you wait until you reach that point, those who chose to start where they were would have already cornered your market or community. Start now, start where you are with the skill you have and improve your craft as you go. Take your customers on a journey with you as you discover new and innovative baking techniques and as you work toward mastering them..

It's crucial to trust yourself and seize opportunities promptly. When you feel confident in the quality of your food, consider turning it into a business.

Suggestions for innovative baking projects

Being creative and innovative as a baker isn't always about inventing the latest viral trend. It can be as simple as starting with seemingly simple flavors and layering them to build amazing flavor profiles that blend together to create amazing experiences for your clients.

Once you've mastered the basics you can move on to more complex techniques. Like pralines, gelée and flavored ganaches to give your cakes, treats and baked goods a more sophisticated and high end approach.

When it comes to decorating techniques after mastering the foundational techniques it's time to move on to more complex forms of decor that will set your skill level apart from the competition, incorporate skell sets like, fondant, gumpaste flowers, pastillage, edible lace, the list of skills are endless. Experiment until you find your style and the areas of cake decorating that brings you the most joy and focus on developing your skill in that area.

Showcase of creative and innovative baked goods

A major complaint of many bakers is that the majority of custom cake orders placed with their bakery are not in designs that they find enjoyable to create.

If you're already running your bakery business then you will need to do a bit of work to introduce the design that inspires you to your buying public. If on the other hand you're just starting out then you have an advantage.

Create a portfolio

Build a portfolio around your niche. To give your audience a better understanding of your skill level and area of specialization, create a portfolio based on your niche. Sketch 3-5 cake designs to use as guides and to display your ideas. Include all the decor details you would like to create in your home bakery.

Using dummy cakes to create the sketched designs, these will double as the showpieces for your studio space as well as displays for promotional events .

Plan a photoshoot, if possible hire a professional photographer. Ensure the cake is well lit, clearly displayed and doesn't blend into the background. Get as many photos as possible, detailed, full shots and videos. Incorporate different angles, add props to create beautiful displays.

These designs will build out your portfolio and will be used across your social media and website going forward.

Work with 2-3 clients to create cakes in your chosen niche. Give 110% effort to those orders then request testimonials from your customers.

Systemize Your Cake Business

How to create systems and processes in your cake business.

Schedule a block of time. Find a quiet place. Do the work

We walk through life thinking that we have no time, we wonder how we can add hours to the day when in fact we are just not utilizing our time to its fullest potential.

- What do you need to improve when it comes to your time?
- Have you spent any time planning your year?
- What do you want your year to look like?
- What are your personal goals?
- Your family goals?

- Your vacation goals?
- Your Big money goals?
- Your business goals?
- How much time would you like to take off from work this year?

Pre-Work

In order to make the most effective use of our time it's not just necessary to organize and schedule our work week but we also need to create schedules or routines for our mornings and nights.

Morning Routines

My morning routine sets the tone for my entire day and when I win my morning I win my day. Is your morning/day built around just you or do you have family to consider?

- What does the ideal morning look like for you? What do you have to accomplish to set yourself up to have the most productive day?
- What time do you need to wake up?
- What do you need to achieve before waking others?
- What time do you need to wake everyone else?
- What needs to be done after they're away so that they can also have the most productive day?
- What time do they and you need to be out the door to be on time for school, work, your set activities for the day?
- Will every morning be the same or do you need different schedules/routines for different days of the week for instance weekdays and weekends?

Example of my morning routine

5:00 am - Wake up

5:05am - make my coffee

5:15 - 5:30 - meditate

5:30 - 5:45 - journal

6:00am - wake up everyone else

6:00 - 6:15 am

I make breakfast while Fabian lays out the kid's uniform for the day.

Ariah and Christian make their beds (they are 5 and 7 years old and have been making their beds for about 3 years) (Christian can make his bed perfectly while still half asleep lol)

6:20 - 6:45 am

We all eat breakfast together.

6:45 am - Ariah and Christian brush their teeth and do their morning personal routines

7:20 am - Ariah and Christian are dressed and in the car and Fabian is driving them to school

7:20 - 8: 00 am

During this time I shower, dress for work and pack my bags

8:00 - 8:20 am Fabian does the same

8:30 am Fabian drives me to work then follows his schedule for his day

This is just our morning routines, it may vary slightly during the week but we try to stick as closely to this schedule as possible.

Assignment - Create your morning routine. Be as detailed as possible

Nighttime routine

- When structuring your evening/nighttime routine are you planning for you or you and others?
- What time does your workday end? What time is theirs (work, school etc)?
- Do you need to pick up your kids from school or do they get dropped off?
- Do you have to make a snack?

- Do you have to make dinner? Or is it already prepped and just needs to be reheated or finished?
- Do you, your partner or kids have after work/school activities?
- Is homework everyday or only certain days?
- What time does screen time end?
- What time is bathtime?
- What Time is bedtime/storytime?

Prepping for the morning

- Do you need to pack for yourself or your family? Snack, lunch, school/work bag?
- Does the electronics need to be plugged in? (laptops, phones etc)

Assignment - Create your nighttime routine. Be as detailed as possible

Structure and Framework

What are your work hours for the day? For us as home bakers this is especially important. If you don't have a set of hours that you work as a business every day then you will end up working 14, 16, 18 even 20 hour days. (telling you this from brutal experience)

Block out your vacation days or weeks for the year. It is important to plan around the major events that will occur during the year.

Of key importance are your personal and family obligations. What personal appointments or obligations do you have in the coming months? Doctor? Dentist? Massages? What are the obligations/appointments of your partner and or children? After work, after school, doctor, dentist etc? When planning and structuring your days, weeks, months and year it's important to be as prepared as possible.

You don't want to schedule a wedding cake delivery during your son's karate belt test (ok, ok in my defense the wedding was on the books for months when the testing dates were selected and I spent as much time as I could in attendance before heading to delivery) ensure that all of these appointments and obligations are added to your schedule.

List all of the major recurring responsibilities that MUST get done on a weekly or monthly basis, in your cake business. Some of mine are business financials, checking the week's orders, breaking the orders into tasks, inventory, marketing, shopping for missing ingredients, making decor pieces, baking etc.

What are the needle moving tasks in your business, these are the tasks that will lead to growth and move your business forward. Admin, marketing etc. as cake designers we always seem to be in reaction mode. Working all the hours of the day, taking little to no breaks, sending all emails on one day, social media and marketing happens when we have a moment to spare.

However if admin and market does not take precedence we may have orders this week but no orders for the following one to three weeks. In order to have consistent orders in our business we need to do admin and client follow up daily. We need to be sure that our products are in front of our ideal costumes daily so that our businesses are at the front of mind when they are ready to order cakes or baked goods for their events.

A general breakdown for me includes:

- Admin - this includes emails, quotes, invoices, client follow up etc. (I set aside one hour per day for admin. Typically before starting on the days tasks)
- Social media posts - Pre scheduled for the day or week including captions, hashtags, posting time etc.
- Monday - Prep day- recipes (pre measuring all dry ingredients) making decor pieces (this is broken down daily in order of importance)
- Tuesday - Baking day - baking all the flavors needed for the weeks orders
- Wednesdays - make all buttercreams and fillings
- Thursday - Assembling all cakes, fill, chill, buttercream
- Friday- Fondant day- cover and decorate all fondant cakes
- Friday - Sunday - Deliveries and Pick-up (create a schedule from first to last pickup, don't forget check ins with clients to ensure timely pickups and delivers)
- Everyday - basically everything you do can be recorded and the video footage used for marketing

Assignment - Create a list of all the tasks that need to be done in your cake business during your work day. Be as detailed as possible

---

Time Blocks - Think about each task and what day and time can you allocate to each.

Example: I have created cake prep Mondays. On Mondays I review cake orders for the week and prep the dry ingredients for each order in preparation for baking Tuesday.

Task: example: Prep the dry ingredients for 2 recipes of vanilla cake

---

When can I do this consistently? Please indicate DAY, TIMEBLOCKS & FREQUENCY examples (which day of the week, month etc.)

BREAK DOWN EACH TASK INTO A SET OF STEPS. This is now your process for completing that task.

Key Tip: create a checklist for each task

Step-By-Step process

ARE YOU SURE THAT YOU HAVE TO DO IT ALL?

Or can you train and DELEGATE?

Create a list of the tasks you will like to stop doing

I have to admit that when it comes to my cake business I am a control freak. For so long I thought that I had to complete every task myself. Even after hiring a part time assistant I just waited all day for her to leave so that I could remake/redo whatever tasks I had assigned her during the day. CRAZY I KNOW!

I had to learn that if I trained her to do the task the correct way then there would be no reason to remake anything. By delegating I was shocked by my ability to stop working in my business and start working on my business. My cake business was finally able to start growing.

_____

_____

_____

It's not enough to just delegate and train fulltime or parttime staff. Also of vital importance is establishing the schedule that everyone in your company will follow day in and day out. What are the major activities and does each person/employee in your cake business know what they should be doing each day of the week based on the breakdown created above?

Organize your team (For each team member)

It bears noting that when hiring an assistant I neither need or could afford her lol. She is the family member of a dear friend and well my friend just wore me down until I agreed to hire her. I didn't have the slightest clue of how to utilize, train or just foster her potential. When I had time to train her I couldn't afford to pay her and when I could afford to pay her I didn't have time to train her. It was a vicious circle and continued for far longer than I would like to admit. She spent her days making pieces and I spent my nights fixing them. I believed that I had to do and make everything myself and I just had to be the best.

I finally started delegating small tasks and training her to do them. I watched as she opened up, learnt to trust her creativity, experiment and add her own personal flarer to the things she was allowed to do.

With that a bond of trust formed and delegated more. I set aside entire weeks for training and making sure that she was comfortable with the tasks assigned. Now we coexist and both handle the tasks that are best suited to our strengths then combine our efforts for the final decor as we compliment each other's strengths and weaknesses.

- What task is this team member responsible for completing? Daily?
- What are the steps necessary to complete each task?
- When does it need to be completed?
- What are the expected outcomes? Daily? Weekly? Monthly?

Assignment - Create systems and processes for each team member and for every task that needs to be completed.

Time management

It is important to constantly audit your time and the time of your team members.

Audit your time over a 24 hour period, then do it over 7 days.

Once you have figured out where time is being "wasted" , adjust the time blocks assigned to the tasks where the time is being wasted.

Biggest culprits for time wasting:

- Social media
- TV
- Talking with friends.

Audit your week

What went well? Why?

What went wrong? Why?

How can we add more of what went well?

What can we do to fix what went wrong? Is more training needed? More structure?

Ensure that speed and accuracy is top of mind and being executed in order to maximize productivity

Put it in your calendar!

I use google calendar, which syncs with my Honeybook calendar's booking system. Please be aware that if it's not scheduled on your calendar it just won't be done!

Streamlining operations and keeping their home bakery space clean is key to operating a legal home bakery. This business comes with spot inspections from your county health inspectors no notice is given meaning that your space needs to be ready at all times. If your bakery has serious violations it may have to close until repairs are made and clearance is given by the health department.

As the sole employee of your business, create a detailed schedule for your operations that includes several scheduled cleanup times per day. Keep the refrigerator and freezer clean, spot check temperatures to make sure they are within allowable variances. Know what the health codes are and enforce them.

CHAPTER 11: ADVANCED BAKING TECHNIQUES

Introduction to more advanced baking techniques for those who want to take their baking to the next level.

Learn to make our featured gardenia sugar flower

Tools

- Rolling pin
- Scissors
- Needle tool
- Tiny scissors
- Pliers
- Tape cutter
- Lear vainer
- Rose vainer
- Floral tape
- Wires- 20,26,28
- Calyx cutter
- Ball tool
- Foam sponge
- Tylose
- Foam tray
- X-Acto knife
- Various sizes of dusting brushes

Petal Dust

- Crystal colors- Pine green
- Crystal colors- Lime green
- Crystal colors-Royal blue
- Crystal colors-Moss green
- Crystal colors-Hunter green

Gardenia

Prepping the Gum Glue

In a container combine ¼ tsp of Tylose powder and 1/8 cup of boiling water

Prepping the wire

Step 1- Cut a 20 gauge wire 5 inches long

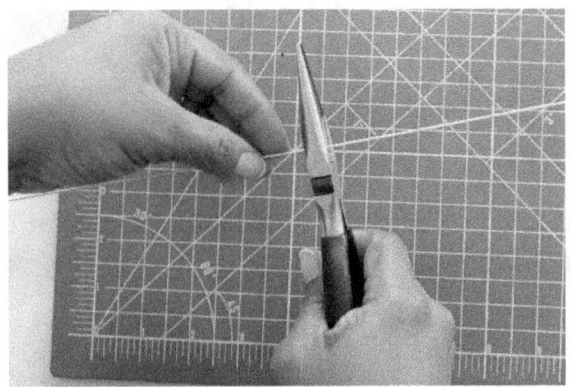

Step 2- Using a needle nose plier's bend one end of the wire to create a hook.

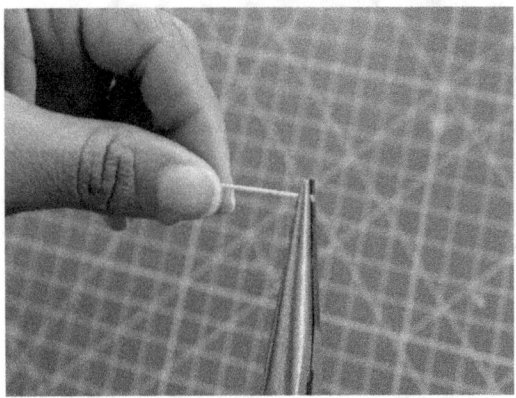

Step 3- Use the pliers to squeeze the hook closed.

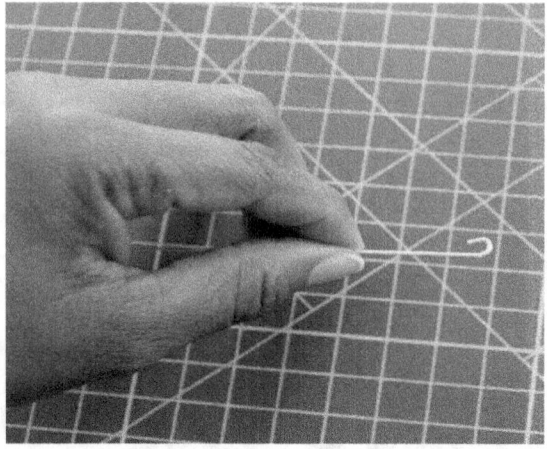

Step 4- Use a tape cutter to cut the florist tape in half. Stretch the tape to activate the glue.

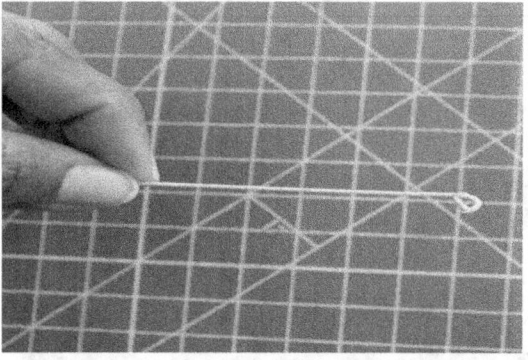

Step 5- Wrap the tape around the hook 5 times.

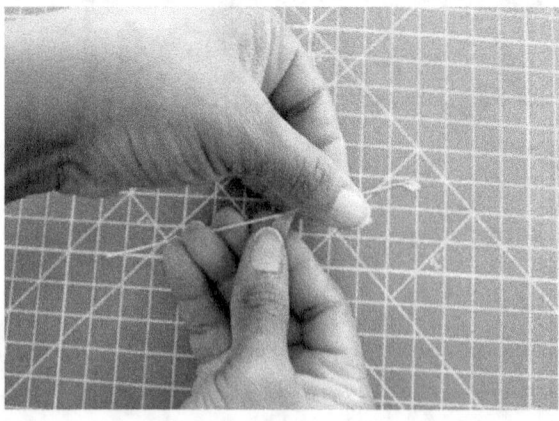

Step 6- Tape down the wire.

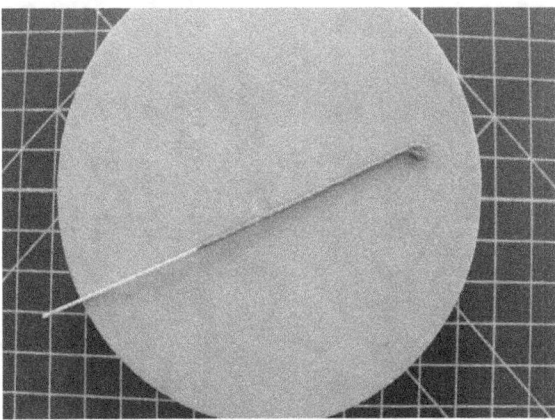

Create the center

Step 7- Soften a small amount of gum paste, then using the palm of your hand roll it into a ball then create a cone shape by rolling one end into a point.

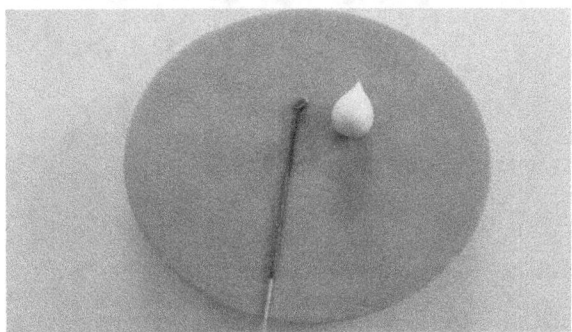

Step 8- Dip the hooked end of the taped wire into the gum glue then wipe off the excess.

Step 9-Insert the hook half way into the cone then pinch the bottom to close tightly around the inserted hook.

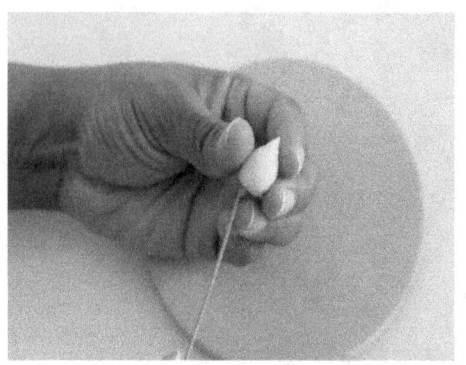
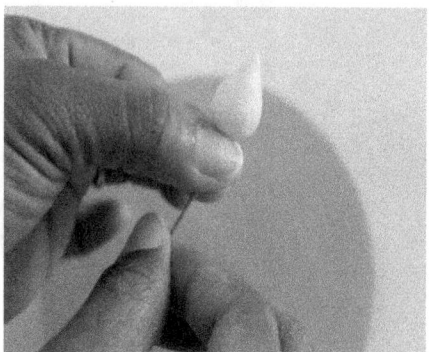

First row of petals

Step 10- Roll a piece of gum paste until thin enough to almost see through. Cut 4 petals using the 1 ¼ inch rose cutter.

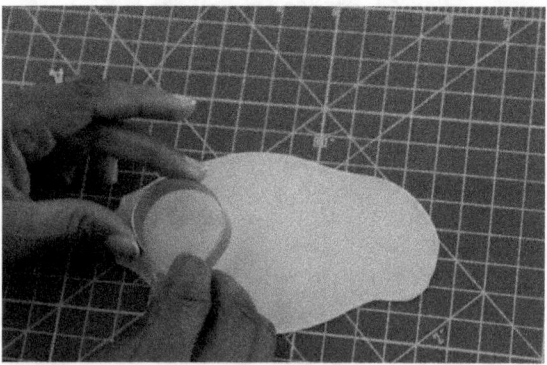

Step 11- Place the petal on a foam pad; place the ball tool half on the edge of the petal and half on the foam pad, press down and roll to soften the edge. Repeat around the entire petal.

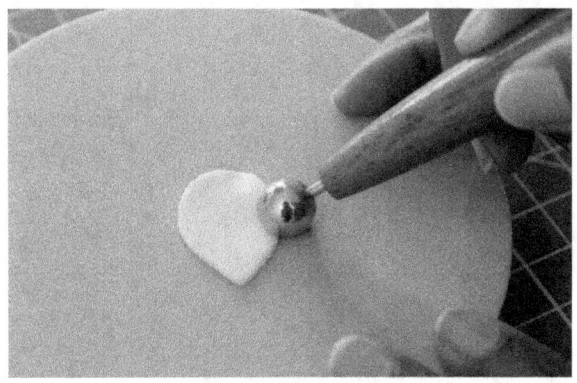

Step 12- Place the softened petal in the vainer and press to vain. Repeat for all 4 petals.

Step 13- Use a needle tool to curl the edges of the petals (roll one edge toward the back of the petal and one toward the front) giving them movement and life.

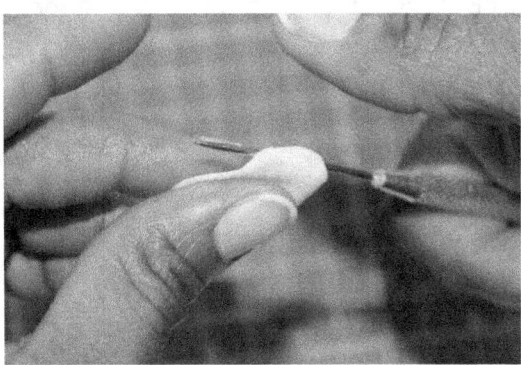

Step 14- Place the petal in the palm of your hand or a soft foam pad. Place the ball tool in the center of the petal, press down and pull to create a curve.

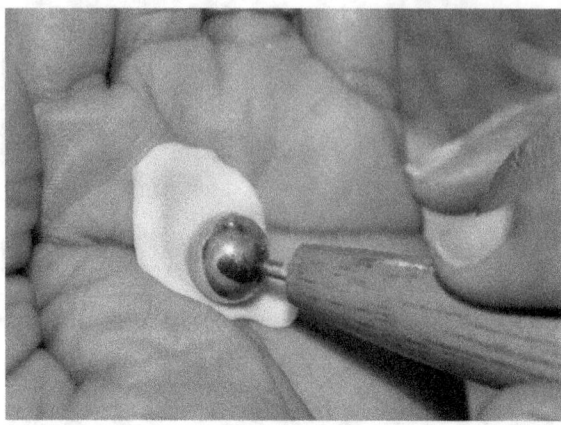

Step 15- Brush the center cone with gum glue.

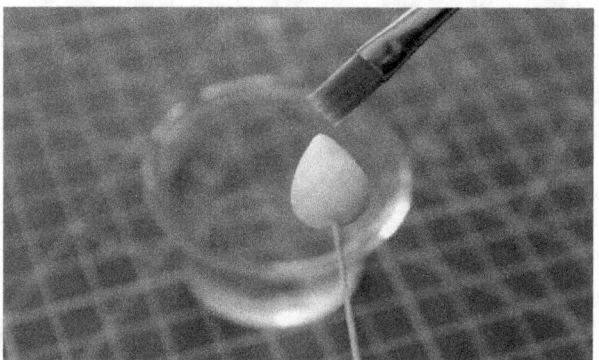

Step 16- Place one petal against the cone, press against the center and curl one end to attach leaving one end open.

Step 17- Tuck a second petal into the space created by the open half of the first petal.

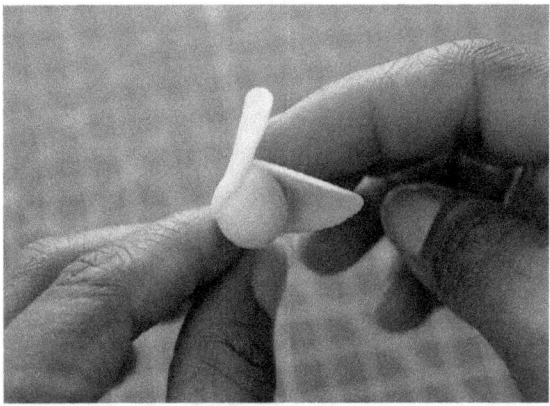

Step 18- Tuck the 3rd petal into the space created by the 2nd petal. Close the petals at the bottom and using a needle tool or your figure gently curl the open petal backwards giving the petals an open look.

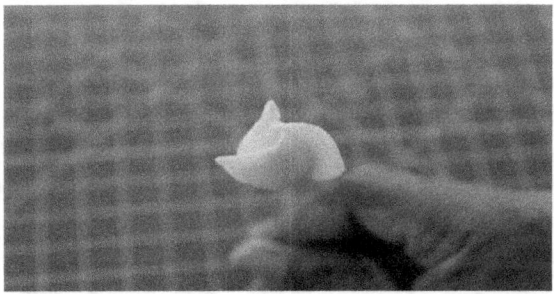

Step 19- Lightly brush the bottom edges of the 4th petal, place against the first petal then curve around to attach.

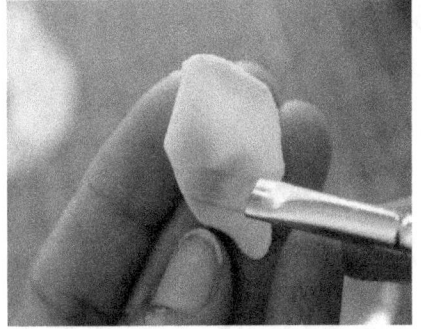

Second row of petals

Step 20- Cut 6 pieces of 28g wire 3" long

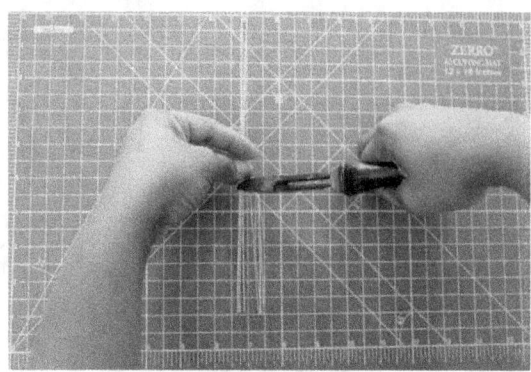

Ridge method Step 21- Roll a large piece of gum paste into a log. Flatten with a rolling pin. Create a ridge in the center by rolling from the center outwards on both sides until almost see through.

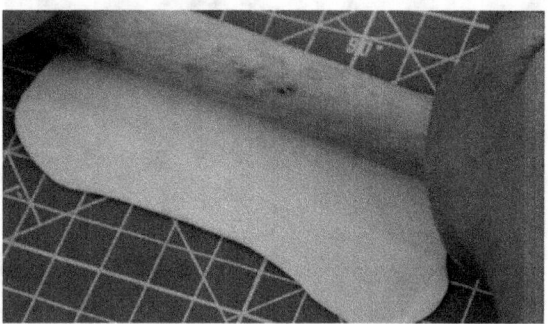

Step 22- Using the 1 ¾ inch rose cutter cut 6 petals.

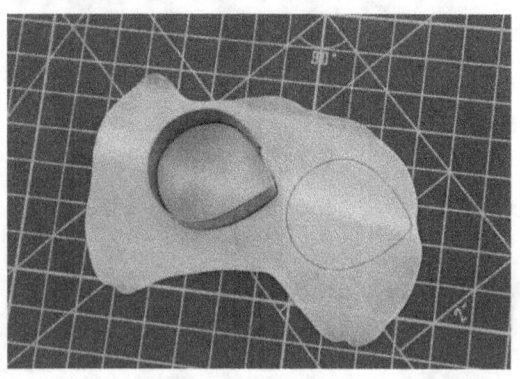

Step 23- dip wire in glue and wipe off excess then holding the petal between the thumb and index finger gently insert the wire 1/3 of the way into the ridge.

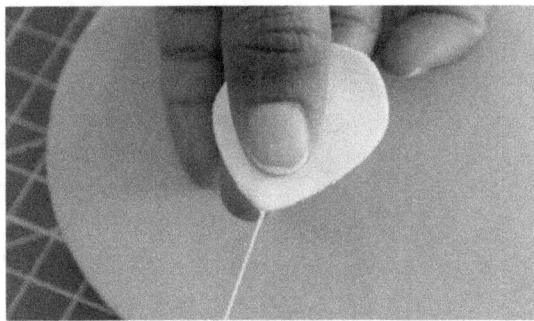

Step 24- Place the petal on a foam pad. Place the ball tool half on the edge of the petal and half on the foam pad, press down and roll to soften the edge. Repeat around the entire petal.

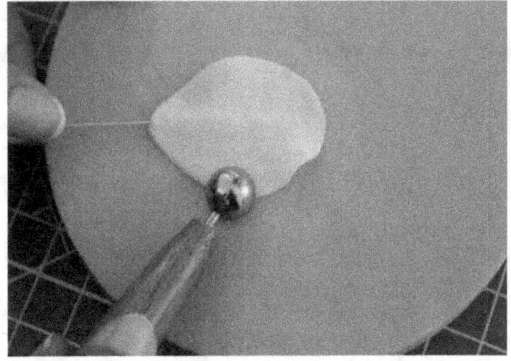

Step 25- Place the softened petal in the vainer and press to vain. Repeat for all 6 petals.

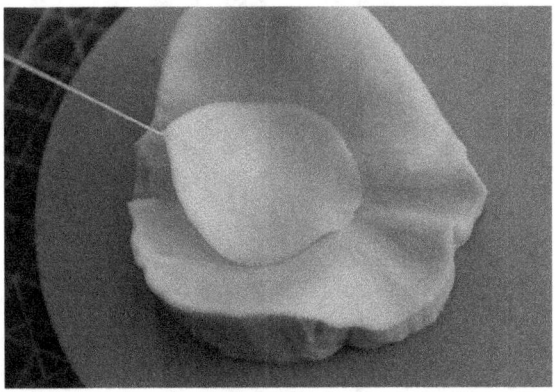

Step 26- Use a needle too to curl the edges of the petals (roll one edge toward the back of the petal and one toward the front) giving them movement and life.

 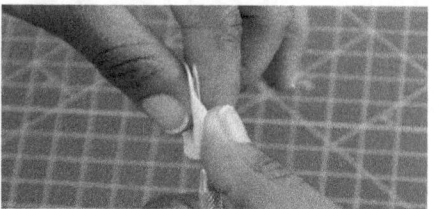

Step 27- Place on a foam tray to dry for a few hours or overnight.

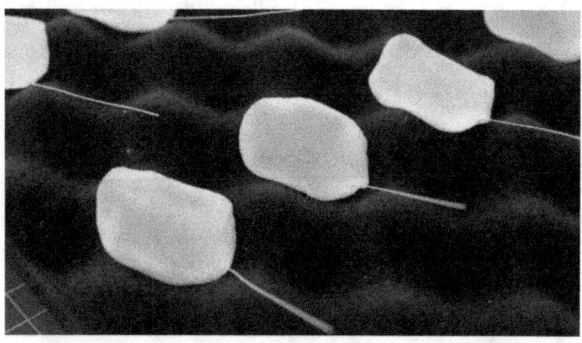

Step 28- Place the petals together in sets of 3 and tape the wires together.

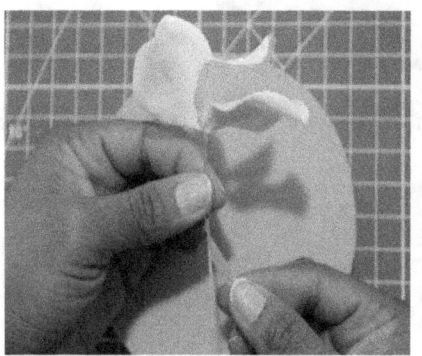 

Step 29- Holding one set of petals and the gardenia bud tape together with florist tape. Repeat the steps using the 2nd set of petals.

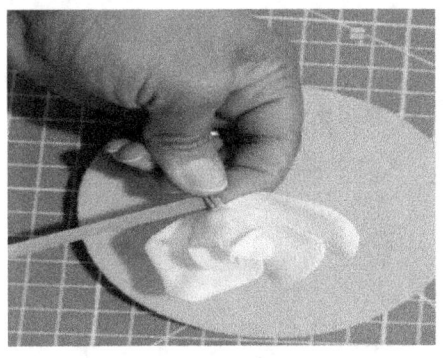 

(For a medium Gardenia stop here)

Third row of petals

Step 30 -Using the 2 ½ inches rose petal cutter repeat the steps above creating 6 petals.

 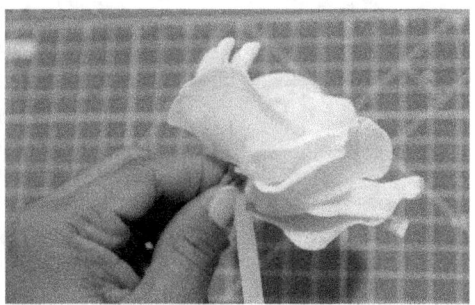

Dusting the Gardenia

Step 31-Using green petal dust mix in a cornstarch to lighten, mix in a very small amount of brown and yellow.

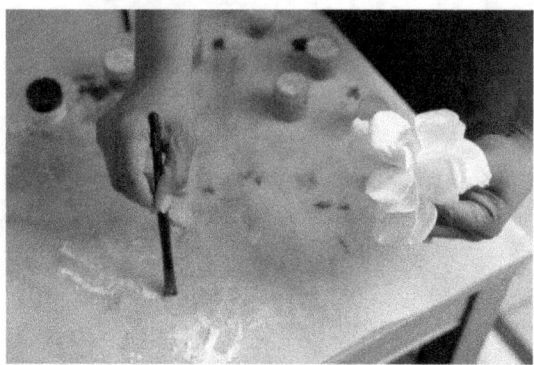

Step 32- Brush the color along the base of each petal, front and back. Brush along edges and in the curves created with the needle tool to create shadows and help bring life to the flower.

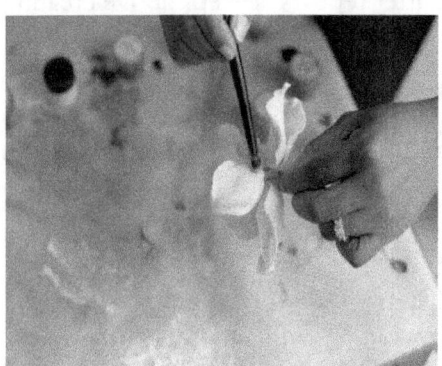

Recipes

Lavender Honey Cake

Layers of lavender cake, soaked in rosemary simple syrup and layered with honey buttercream and covered in either honey swiss meringue or vanilla swiss meringue buttercream

Lavender cake - (lavender milk - ¼ cup whole milk + 2 tablespoons food grade lavender, heated for 5 min then allowed to cool then strained) Add 1-2 drops of lavender food color into the milk and fully dissolve.

Rosemary simple syrup (equal parts water and sugar + rosemary)

1 cup water

1 cup granulated sugar

4-5 sprigs of rosemary

Combine in a pot, heat until sugar dissolves then allow to boil for 5-10 minutes or until the rosemary flavors the syrup

Honey buttercream

2 sticks unsalted butter

2 cups powdered sugar, sifted, spooned and leveled

¾ cups of honey (add ¼ cup at a time, objective: attain a honey flavor without being to sweet or compromising the integrity of the buttercream)

1 tsp vanilla bean paste

2 tablespoons heavy whipping cream

Pinch of salt pinch - 1-8 tsp

Vanilla Cake

Ingredients

- 2 1/2 cups cake flour
- 2 cups sugar
- ¾ cup sour cream
- 2 sticks butter (1 cup)
- 1/8 cup vegetable oil
- 1 3/4 teaspoon baking powder
- 1/2 teaspoon baking soda
- 1 teaspoon vanilla
- 1/2 teaspoon vinegar
- 1/2 teaspoon salt
- 4 extra-large eggs

- 1 cup buttermilk
- 1/4 teaspoon nutmeg (optional)
- 1/4 teaspoon cinnamon (optional)

Butter or spray the cake pans add parchment round to the bottom of the pan, then flour.

Method

1. Place the rack in the center of the oven and preheat at 350 degrees F for 20 minutes.

2. Sieve the following dry ingredients together (cake flour, baking powder, baking soda, salt, nutmeg and cinnamon) mix by hand until thoroughly incorporated.

3. To the mixing bowl add sugar butter and oil. Mix until it becomes light, fluffy and approximately doubled in volume. Approximately 8 to 10 minutes.

Note: for cupcakes

¾ fill each cupcake cup. Let the batter rest for 10 minutes. Bake for 18 minutes or until the inserted tester is clean when removed. Remove from the over place on the cooling rack and allow to cook to room temperature. Tip Filling the cupcake cups more than halfway will cause the batter to overflow when baking.

4. Add eggs one at a time making sure each is fully incorporated before adding the next.

5. Add vanilla and beat for an additional minute

6. Add sour cream and beat for an additional minute

7. Transfer mixture from mixing bowl into a large bowl

8. Add dry ingredients in 3 parts and wet ingredients in 2 to the sugar mixture, alternating between wet and dry. Fold ingredients to combine after each addition (starting with dry and ending with dry).

9. Divide the batter evenly between pans

10. Let batter rest for 10 minutes

11. Bake for 30 to 35 minutes or until the inserted tester is clean when removed.

12. Remove from oven and let cake cool in pan for 5 min

13. Run an offset spatula along the edge of the cake pan to loosen any stuck areas

14. To remove from the pan place a piece of parchment paper on a cake board and put it on top of the cake pan, then holding tightly flip the pan over allowing the cake to smoothly slip out and land on the parchment paper after lifting the pan off. Place a second cake board to the bottom and flip right side up. Place cake on a cooling rack until room temperature.

15. Refrigerate or freeze until ready to decorate.

SWISS MERINGUE BUTTERCREAM RECIPE

Process

Tools

- Wire strainer
- Rubber scraper
- Large heat proof bowl
- Mixing bowl
- Whip attachment
- Paddle attachment
- Measuring cups
- Measuring spoons
- Half and half Vinegar & water mixture.

Prep:

- Cut butter into 1 tablespoon cubs. Add the cubs to a bowl.
- Measure out all ingredients including the extract.

- Wash/wipe ALL utensils with the vinegar and water mixture. This removes grease from your utensils.

Tip

Grease prevents meringue from fully developing

Ingredients

4 sticks of unsalted butter	453.6g unsalted butter
2 ¾ cups of sugar	552.4g sugar
2 pinches of salt	1.48g salt
1 ¼ cups egg whites	303.8g
1 TBSP vanilla extract	13g
1 tsp vinegar (optional)	4.8g

Instructions

1. Separate the egg whites from the yolks. Separate one at a time into a small bowl then place each egg white into a measuring cup.

Tip: This prevents the addition of bad eggs and from contaminating the entire batch.

2. Place the egg whites, sugar, vinegar and salt into a large heat safe bowl.

3. Create a "Bain Marie" by placing the heat safe bowl over a simmering pan of water. Make sure the bowl is not touching the water.

4. Stir until sugar is dissolved and mixture comes to approximately 140°F. If you're not using a thermometer, sugar should be dissolved and no graininess felt when rubbed between two fingers. It will be hot to the touch.

Tip: Keep a constant eye during this step. The egg white can be easily cooked if left unattended. DO NOT WALK AWAY

Tip

Egg whites are pasteurized (heated to destroy bacteria), but not cooked, by bringing them to 140° F and keeping them at that temperature for approximately 3 1/2 minutes.

5.   Remove from heat and strain into a mixing bowl.

Tip: straining the mixture helps with the following-

- Prevents small pieces of cooked eggs from getting into your meringue.
- Prevents larger clumps or particles of undissolved sugar from getting into the meringue.

6.   Immediately place the bowl on the stand mixer, add the whip attachment. Whip starting on slow speed then gradually increasing speed to medium-high. Whip until meringue becomes thick, glossy and forms a stiff peak. Continue to whip the meringue until the bowl feels cool to the touch, approximately 15 minutes. (set the timer for 15 minutes then adjust as needed)

7.   Switch the whisk attachment to the paddle attachment. With the mixer on low, add the butter a few tablespoons at a time, beating until smooth after each addition.

8.   Once all the butter has been incorporated, mix in vanilla extract. If needed, continue beating until smooth.

Storage

Swiss meringue buttercream may be stored on the counter for 2 days, 1 week in the refrigerator or 1 month in the freezer. If storing in the refrigerator or freezer, bring to room temperature then re-whip before using.

Trouble Shoot

Soupy buttercream

If after the addition of all the butter the buttercream won't come together, refrigerate for 20 minutes then whip for 5 minutes. If your buttercream is very warm this process may need to be repeated until the buttercream comes together. (LAST SENTENCE NEEDS SOME WORK)

Curdled buttercream

If your buttercream is cold, place your mixing bowl over a water bath "Bain Marie", heat for a few minutes (1-2 minutes at a time) until the outer layer of buttercream melts then whip. Repeat until the desired consistency is achieved.

Crystallized buttercream

Crystallized buttercream is when sugar crystals sugar reforms. How can you tell if your buttercream crystallized? If the buttercream feels gritty when rubbed between your fingers or eaten.

The addition of the vinegar to this recipe helps prevent the sugar from crystallizing.

Tip: melt your buttercream until the sugar dissolves then re whip

Unfortunately I have never had any luck with fixing crystallized buttercream. After countless hours I usually start over. In the event that this happens I suggest starting making another batch of buttercream.

CHAPTER 12: FACING CHALLENGES AND OVERCOMING OBSTACLES

Practical advice on how to handle common challenges and obstacles in the baking business

Self-taught bakers and cake decorators often experience difficulty when training and developing their staff which lets face it is you, you are the staff. Developing your fundamental baking and decoration techniques is the best way to stand out in the current landscape of the baking industry which has been made popular by the many television shows and streaming services.

Develop your skill and business by taking classes and courses. Do some research to determine the way you learn best, in-person, online, books, pdf's.

As the sole employee of your business you need to be knowledgeable of both the front of house and backhouse of your business. Meaning that you need to be able to answer questions about why using fresh ingredients like eggs, butter and milk produces a better bakery product while as a back of house employee you need to be able to correctly measure your ingredients and follow recipe directions. Remember baking is a science. You need to know your products. How the ingredients work together, which ingredients work best for you, how your batter tastes, how it smells while baking and the taste and moisture content that should be expected after baking. When you know your products inside out you can effectively explain it to others.

Another frequent difficulty may be product quality and consistency. The solution to this problem is practicing and ensuring that you follow the recipe precisely. Using a scale instead of cups will help with accurate measurements facilitating consistent results when baking. A menu item should not be added until you can regularly produce it in all the various sizes that you offer with consistent quality, meaning consistent taste, texture, moisture etc. this gives your bakery an edge and helps you to stand out in the baking industry.

Streamlining operations and keeping their home bakery space clean is key to operating a legal home bakery. This business comes with spot inspections from your county health inspectors no notice is given meaning that your space needs to be ready at all times. If your bakery has serious violations it may have to close until repairs are made and clearance is given by the health department.

As the sole employee of your business, create a detailed schedule for your operations that includes several scheduled cleanup times per day. Keep the refrigerator and freezer clean, spot check temperatures to make sure they are within allowable variances. Know what the health codes are and enforce them.

Marketing challenges in home bakery business. If no one knows your bakery exists no one can buy from you. You need to utilize social media sites like Instagram, Facebook and twitter as well as search engines such as YouTube to keep your customers up to date on new products as well as any upcoming sales. Check that your business is listed on all available listing sites. Choose an advertising platform that best aligns with the needs of your business.

Using social media as a marketing tool poses many challenges as it is a whole other job on its own. Don't get me started on the 5 am scrolls, the courses /classes bought promising to help develop an understanding of social media and grow a following only to be left disappointed by the course content and utter lack of delivering on the promises made.

After seemingly endless days of baking, cleaning and decorating, we are also photographers and social media marketers. While these tasks are difficult and require a learning curve they are the best means of getting your bakery and baked goods discovered in today's society. Use behind the scenes videos and pictures to keep them engaged and coming back. Be clear in your caption and always use a clear call to action that actually asks for the sale. Ensure that your bio is simple and tells the customer your name, business name, location, jurisdiction, your business services and how they can do business with you. Your contact information should be easy to find.

Creating financial management processes for their home bakery is a difficult but necessary task. Your bakery is a business so in addition to being knowledgeable about the ins and outs of baking you also need to be aware of and implement good financial practices in your business. You need to know your numbers. Knowing exactly what your cakes and baked goods cost to produce gives you a clearer idea of what price you should be changing for them. Always keep in mind that baked goods are a perishable item so if its miss managed and proper baking instructions are not followed they need to be discarded however they still cost the same amount of money to produce. Have frequent financial meetings with yourself, track your spending and orders. Set up at least a basic accounting system or have your account or bookkeeper set it up for you and show you how to use it.

Creating a financial plan for your bakery is the first and most important step to grow your home bakery business. This should include all expenses your bakery will incur monthly, such as rent, utilities, ingredients, delivery fees and your wages. After calculating the monthly cost to run your home bakery, price your cakes and baked goods accordingly to ensure that you will make enough money to cover the cost of running the bakery plus enough to make a profit. There can be no growth in your home bakery business without profit.

As home bakers we also may experience limitations with storage, equipment, and functionality. Lack of storage makes buying ingredients in bulk difficult. It is important to balance storage for your family and business. Dictate specific space in your home for storage. Create detailed labels for containers so that small tools can be easily found. Organization is key to bringing balance to your life and business.

When facing a challenge with inventory management, planning ahead before shopping for weekly or monthly orders helps minimize stress. Cross check your list with current supplies in your home bakery kitchen to avoid over buying and overstocking which would crowd your already limited storage space.

Personal stories of overcoming obstacles

Running a home bakery is a time-consuming, physically and mentally demanding job.

For 14 of the last 16 years I operated as if nothing much beyond the demands of my business mattered and as if my body was an endless resource. My family and friends got the benefit of my leftover energy and I have zero left for myself. Then 2 years ago I worked my body and mind into burnout. This wasn't the rest and recovery type of burnout. This was if you make one more cake in the state you're never touching another cake for life.

I was tired all the time, I woke up tired, went to sleep tired and to this day I'm not even sure how I functioned. This happened at the highest point in my business, while paying 4 part time employees and looking down the barrel of booked out months with orders constantly coming in.

In 14 years I had worked through sickness and health never letting down my clients and hardly taking any downtime for myself. I mean I was back at work one month after having my son and 3 weeks after having my daughter....

I somehow managed to work through the orders already on the books then I went to Fabian and said "Okay, I need a break!) I think he thought I was joking because in 14 years he had never heard me utter those words and in his defense at the time I still thought that a week off from work would solve my problems. Lol boy was I wrong.

I scheduled the week off and decided to use the time to clean and organize the studio. So the week off became work then after work there was dinner, bath time, story time with the kids. Endless tasks with no rest in sight.

It all came to a head when I could barely make myself get out of bed in the mornings. I stopped taking orders and tried to rest. The problem was that for 14 years I had worked nonstop and now my body had no idea how to rest or what rest even looked like.

Then came the added mental stress. My brain just couldn't let go of the fact that I was at home not working, living off my savings and my bills still needed to be covered.

Nights were the most intense. I woke up in a panic every night for months soaked in sweat. I would change then sit in the dark for hours.

I had worked my mind and body to the point that it felt physically broken. I lived in a sense of panic that I would never be the same and would never be able to return to my business life with the same energy and creativity that seemed so effortless in the past.

Overcoming and getting back to some sense of norm would take time and work. It would take time because it was clear that just taking a break wasn't working and it would take work because I needed to dial into my life and business, find or create balance, then build a schedule around that. What are the demands of my family life? What are the demands of my job? What do I need to do personally and what could I delegate to others? What needed my absolute attention. How many cakes could I optimally produce in a week? How much do I need to make to cover my bills, maintain our quality of life while working less hours and taking less orders? Yes, like I said the work had just begun. I had to create an entire production schedule that got my orders done on time, optimally the night before delivery with delivery days scheduled for Saturdays and Sundays.

While working through these issues I still had to deal with the mental and physical exhaustion. For months working for even a few hours a day exhausted me. I scheduled a checkup with my doctor, added vitamins customized to my body and fixed my diet. Yes that meant making separate meals for myself and my family but that's ok as I started feeling healthier.

I have always exercised, in fact I attribute the fact that my body didn't just give out to the fact that for years I did some form of workout but now it was time to get serious. I hired a trainer and very honestly explained my life, my body, the demands of my life and business and what I needed to function optimally then we got to work. Strength training has been one of the greatest life savers for me in recent years but for the sake of honesty and 100 percent transparency after 2 years it still feels like I'm working back to what feels normal. While late nights are few and far between for me now, the very possibility of it can trick my body into believing that I'm reverting to a life of constant work and strain.

My journey working back to health and mental stability has been long, hard and quite frankly expensive. I have doubled down on therapy, journaling, meditating, exercising and continued to eat healthier. I created more balance with my work and family life. I decluttered my space at home and at work and streamlined as many processes as possible. Delegation, detailed production schedules at work and limiting last min orders have made for a better quality of life.

Recognizing our mistakes and missteps as home bakery owners isn't always easy but when they come to our attention it's our business to make the corrections necessary to avoid the issues in the future.

Competition from well-known bakers and existing brands

From the beginning of my career as a cake designer I was obsessed. I spent every spare hour working to become better. Tweaking recipes, learning to be consistent, learning to perfect my buttercream and fondant the list was endless. To say that I was conscious of other bakers as competition, I honestly say that it never occurred to me. I focused instead on the bakers I admired and the parts of our craft they excelled at that I hoped to someday become proficient at or even master. I wanted cleanly professionally finished cakes, not sweaty, melting messes. I wanted to fix my problem with bulging cakes and embrace my obsession with sharp edges. My first inkling that I had not only started to build a brand but that my business had earned a reputation based on taste, value and consistency was when I got a call from the W Hotel, I had been recommended to them to be a contractor for their event cakes. Ultimately we weren't a good fit but it was shocking to me that without it being my focus while just really working to perfect my craft I had built a business that had a life and really existed outside of Alana the person.

It's still surprising how many people know of my business, have had my cakes or know someone who has ordered from me. I still love and can't get enough of the calls that start off with "10 years ago I went to a birthday party and had your carrot cake, do you still make THAT carrot cake". It really reinforces the ground work I did in an effort to build a business that at the time I didn't realize I was doing. I hadn't given any thought to the possibility that it could become an entity that outlived me, could be sold or could serve my family as a legacy long after I'm no longer here.

Now that I am aware of the reputation of my business I do all I can to foster and build upon it. To make my clients feel welcomed, really listen and take to heart the issues they are facing and find solutions to their problems. Those things and so much more helps set me apart from the competition.

Not charging what I'm worth or the value of my cakes

I didn't have the slightest clue of how to begin pricing my cakes and baked goods. I made 6/7 cakes per week plus cupcakes and cookies and I still couldn't cover my bills. All of this while being considered expensive for a home baker.

I had to really learn to dial in and figure out what it was costing me to produce the cakes I made. Learn to charge for making all the detailed handmade decor pieces. To value and account for not just my time but the time of my assistant. For years I paid her but never paid myself. I just didn't charge enough to be able to afford to do both.

Creating detailed baking, production and construction processes and timelines helped me to account for each step of the process as well as document and account for our time. Now my cakes are valued in a way that I can make more from 1-2 cake orders per week than I did making 6/7 cakes and living in a state of constant rush and overwhelm.

Learning how to utilize and train an assistant

It bears noting that when hiring an assistant I neither need nor could afford her lol. She is the family member of a dear friend and well my friend just wore me down until I agreed to hire her. I didn't have the slightest clue of how to utilize, train or just foster her potential. When I had time to train her I couldn't afford to pay her and when I could afford to pay her I didn't have time to train her. It was a vicious circle and continued for far longer than I would like to admit. She spent her days making pieces and I spent my nights fixing them. I believed that I had to do and make everything myself and I just had to be the best.

I finally started delegating small tasks and training her to do them. I watched as she opened up, learnt to trust her creativity, experiment and add her own personal flarer to the things she was allowed to do.

With that a bond of trust formed and delegated more. I set aside entire weeks for training and making sure that she was comfortable with the tasks assigned. Now we coexist and both handle the tasks that are best suited to our strengths then combine our efforts for the final decor as we compliment each other's strengths and weaknesses.

Encouragement and advice for persistence

For as long as I can remember I have always had the need to "try one more time" as home bakers and cake decorators often with no professional training so many things go wrong. We're often in a constant state of overwhelm or stress trying to fix the things that we break on a daily basis. learn to be patient with yourself and give yourself grace. Understand that there is always a learning curve and everything gets better with time and practice.

We often think that as home bakers we need to operate in a constant state of motivation. However if we create systems, processes and schedules for our business we can operate in a state of consistency when motivation has deserted us. It allows us to keep our business running and to keep working towards our goals.

"Success leaves clues". As home bakers and cake decorators living in the social media age we are constantly bombarded with a litany of other bakers who seem so much more successful or creative that we are. I encourage you not to compare your skill or creativity but to take a look at their business model, learn from them, what's working for them? Can a version of that work for you and your business? How are they showing up for their business and community? Can you emulate that consistency in your business? Take the clues left by their successes and implement it to create a better business model for your business.

Resources to help you grow your baking business

A complimentary Resource Hub featuring tools, exclusive recipes from my personal home bakery, guides, templates, and more. Specifically designed to assist home bakers like yourself in building their own prosperous Home Bakery Business!

Go to https://www.bakingitacademy.com/thehub

Our 6 Week Baker Profit Amplifier program is a group coaching program that gives home bakers step-by-step strategies and over-the-shoulder training showing you exactly how to get more clients, higher profits and streamline your baking operations by creating systems and processes. This program is taught live weekly and begins with an initial assessment of your baking business. We bring in experts like Lawyers and Accounts to ensure that we provide you with the information you need to start and grow a profitable baking business.

Go to https://www.bakingitacademy.com/amplifier

"Pricing like a pro" is an all-encompassing course designed to guide you in adopting a profit-oriented mindset. This course covers essential aspects such as developing the right pricing mentality, comprehending the components of pricing, effectively communicating price adjustments to customers, establishing a distinctive presence in the baking industry, and adeptly managing your financial aspects. As an added bonus, the course features an invaluable pricing calculator that can revolutionize your home baking business. This calculator, constructed as a master tool, allows you to input all relevant information necessary for pricing your cakes. The automated process generates custom quotes, complete with a profit margin calculation and a dedicated section for factoring in special ingredients or decorations.

Go to https://www.bakingitacademy.com/pricinglikeapro

Legal basics for bakers - If you have ever wondered, do I need a contract for my home bakery business? Is my business protected? What clauses should I include? What's a clause? Then Legal basics for bakers is for you. Taught by my attorney, it walks you through everything you need to include in your contract to ensure that your home bakery is legally protected and as a bonus we provide you with a contract template that you can customize for your bakery business.

Go to https://www.bakingitacademy.com/bakingbythebook

Fondant mastery: the sharp edge masterclass is perfect for the decorator who is ready to take their decorating skills to the next level by building their fondant skill. This course sets you up with the foundation to create any fondant design. It helps decorators who "lack confidence" in their fondant skills become confident and increase their productivity. If you're tired of all the frustrations that come with working with fondant. Whether you've been trying to up-level your cake decorating skills for years or your experiences are limited to childhood baking with your mom, Fondant mastery: the sharp edge masterclass can help you Build your confidence, Change how you view yourself, Uplevel you skill and Turn your followers into customers.

Go to https://www.bakingitacademy.com/fondantmastery

The Cake Cost Cruncher™□ was developed as a catalyst for the growth of your baking business. This calculator serves as a precise and comprehensive tool, breaking down all your costs to ensure that each set price not only covers expenses but also incorporates a profit margin, enabling you to increase earnings. With this innovative calculator, you can effortlessly compute ingredients, supplies, overhead, labor, and delivery costs. Gaining a clear view of your costs will transform your approach, instilling confidence in quoting and a genuine understanding of your true expenses. Armed with this knowledge, you can establish a starting price for your products, providing clarity for both yourself and your customers.

Go to https://www.bakingitacademy.com/costcruncher

If you are moving from hobby baking to making baking your main income, our 6-month Baking Business Accelerator Program with get you there fast. Learn to craft a successful business strategy, optimize your product line,and market effectively to build a thriving, 6-figure bakery business. The program includes comprehensive tutorials that guides you through the step-by-step process of leveling, assembling, trimming, crumb coating, and butter-creaming your cake tiers. Unlock the secrets to constructing robust and stable foundations for your cake creations, all from the convenience of your home. Once you've mastered these foundational skills, you'll have the ability to apply them to any cake design. This course ensures that your skills will undoubtedly progress to the next level."

Go to https://www.bakingitacademy.com/bakeit

www.ingramcontent.com/pod-product-compliance
Lightning Source LLC
Chambersburg PA
CBHW071156290526
45796CB00007B/53